THE RHYMNEY RAILWAY

Volume 2

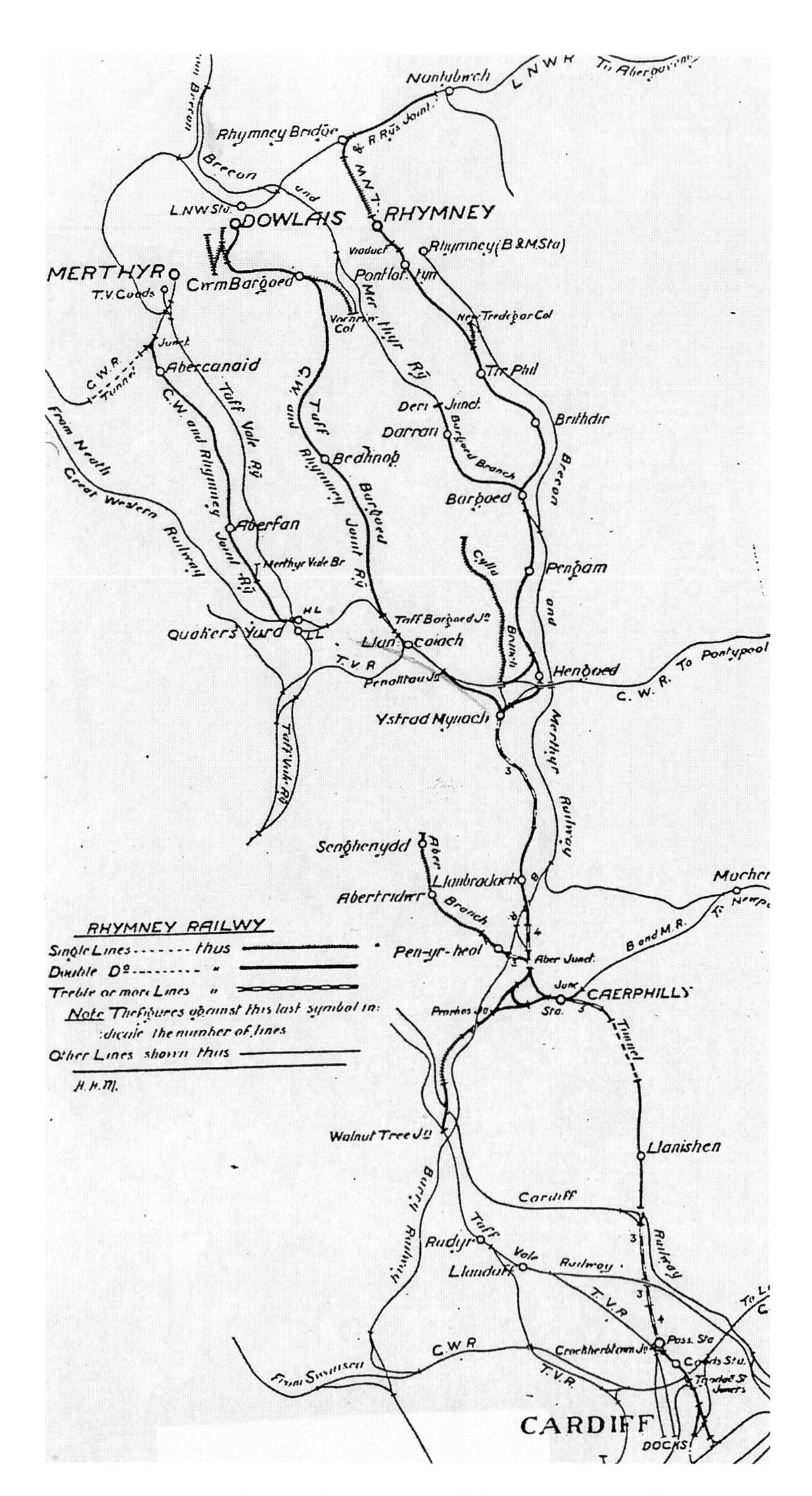

Map of the Rhymney Railway system. *The Railway Magazine*, 1910

THE RHYMNEY RAILWAY

Volume 2
Branch lines in the Valleys

John Hutton

• RAILWAY HERITAGE •
from
The NOSTALGIA Collection

This book is dedicated to my wife's son Brian, her daughter Helen, son-in-law Mike and their family, Jeremy, Bethany and Amber

First published in 2004

British Library Cataloguing in Publication Data

A catalogue record for this book is available from the British Library.

ISBN 1 85794 228 0

Silver Link Publishing Ltd
The Trundle
Ringstead Road
Great Addington
Kettering
Northants NN14 4BW

Tel/Fax: 01536 330588
email: sales@nostalgiacollection.com
Website: www.nostalgiacollection.com

Printed and bound in Great Britain

A Silver Link book
from
The NOSTALGIA *Collection*

Page 1 The Rhymney Railway's seal as used on the side of its carriages. Although the chevrons have faded, much of the fine detail can still be seen.

The coat of arms has an interesting history; taken from the common seal of the company, according to the minutes taken at the first Board Meeting it was decided that it should be arranged as follows: Cardiff arms to the lower right of the seal, Newport arms to the lower left, surmounted by a vignette representing furnaces in the Egyptian style of architecture (this type of furnace was in use in the Rhymney Iron Works in 1828), a colliery on the right, and a ship to the left, to indicate the two terminals of the line. However, the engraver must have misunderstood the intention, for he placed on the left the seal that should have been on the right, and the colours of the Cardiff coat of arms are incorrect, as the chevrons should be gold. The placing of Newport on the shield is a mystery as the Rhymney Railway never went there. One wonders if is inclusion caused the first Marquess of Bute to turn in his grave!

The common seals of the company can be seen at the Great Western Railway Museum, Swindon, together with the seals of other railway companies that were taken over by the GWR both before and after the Grouping of 1922. I am indebted to Mr E. J. Starr, a former railwayman who once worked at the Caerphilly engine and carriage works.

Below Beddau Loop Junction was the point where the Caerphilly branch left the original Rhymney Railway main line between Aber Junction and Walnut Tree Junction. Former GWR engine No 5692 passes the signal box at 10.15am on 17 February 1957 with a Marshalling Sidings to McClaren Colliery empties train. The box closed in 1967, and the '56xx' Class engine, built at Swindon Works in 1927, was withdrawn in 1965. *B. J. Miller collection*

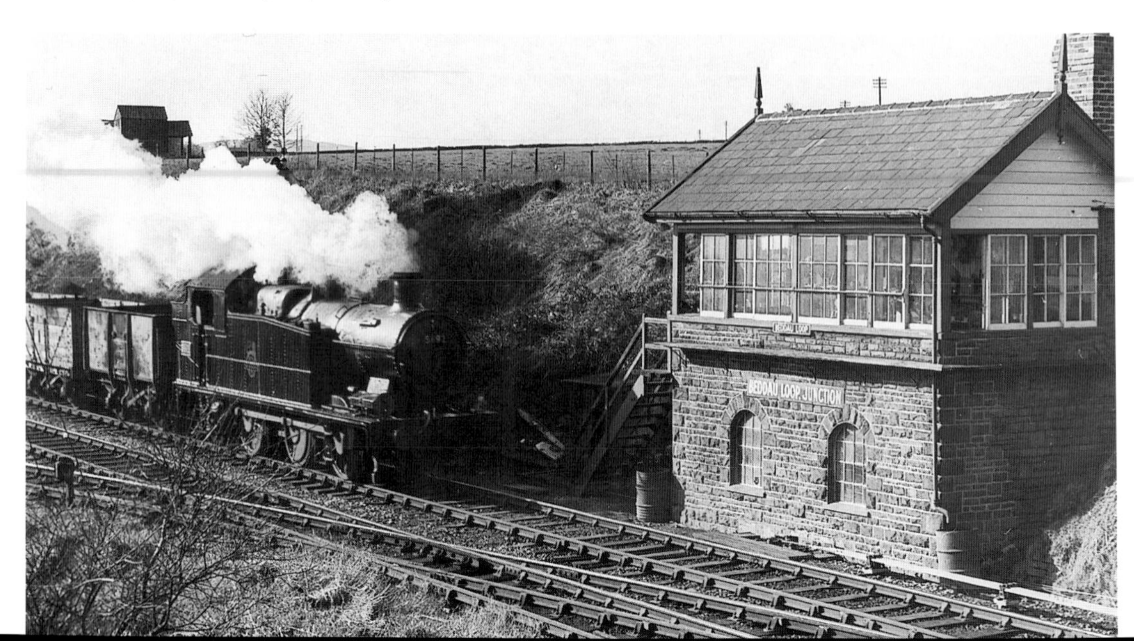

CONTENTS

On the Darran and Deri branch in about 1963, at Ogilvie Colliery Sidings, engine driver Mr Dick Talbot is on the footplate of '56xx' 0-6-2T No 5697, with fellow engine driver Mr Viv Crabb on the ground. The '56xx' engines were used extensively on South Wales valley branch lines, and were good workhorses; this example, built at Swindon Works in 1927, was withdrawn in 1963. *V. Crabb*

Above Dominated by the slag tips, this is Dowlais Cae Harris signal box and engine shed at the head of the Rhymney Railway and Great Western Railway Joint Taff Bargoed branch. *B. J. Miller collection*

Below A general view of Senghenydd station, goods yard and associated collieries at the head of the Aber branch in the early years of the 20th century. *Lens of Sutton collection*

RHYMNEY RAILWAY BRANCHES

A full history of all the Rhymney Railway system is given in Volume 1, which deals principally with the 1871 main line, but since this volume covers the various branches off the main line, it seems worth repeating the relevant historical background here.

The Rhymney Railway from Cardiff to the upper Rhymney Valley was incorporated by an Act of Parliament on 24 July 1854. The line from Rhymney would join the Taff Vale Railway at Walnut Tree Bridge, Taffs Well, and the company would have running powers over the TVR to the junction at Crockherbtown, Cardiff. After delays arising from the nature of the land, the Walnut Tree branch was finally opened on 25 February 1858 for goods, and 31 March for passengers.

The Act also included two other elements. One was the making of a branch from Aber, the site of the first Caerphilly station, to coal workings at Wernddu. The other was the authorising of a branch from Crockherbtown to terminate at a new dock in course of construction, authorised by the trustees of the Marquess of Bute and called Bute East Dock; this line was some 1½ miles long from Crockherbtown, and 5 miles and 71 chains from Walnut Tree Bridge. The dock branch opened in September 1857, but the only traffic was freight via the Taff Vale Railway until the line to Walnut Tree Bridge was opened.

In 1860 the Caerphilly branch was opened, extending eastward 1½ miles from Penrhos Junction to Caerphilly town. Much of the one million cubic yards of hard-won material from the Nantgarw cutting on the Walnut Tree branch was used in its foundations.

In 1862 the London & North Western Railway leased the Merthyr, Tredegar & Abergavenny Railway, and gained parliamentary sanction on 25 July 1864 to build jointly with the Rhymney Railway a line from Rhymney to Rhymney Bridge, with the Rhymney company having running powers to Nantybwch, a joint station on the MT&A line. In return this agreement gave the LNWR running powers from Walnut Tree Bridge to Crockherbtown. It was clear that the LNWR was looking to Cardiff docks, for included in the 1864 Act was a new line of railway from Caerphilly to Cardiff; without doubt it was the LNWR's much-needed financial help that would make this possible. The new main line was double track from its opening, on 1 April 1871, the distance overall from Rhymney to Cardiff being shortened by 1½ miles.

On 5 September 1871 the Rhymney Bridge branch was ceremonially opened; from Rhymney to Rhymney Bridge it was single line, but from there to Nantybwch it was double track. Passenger services began on 2 October 1871.

The third notable line to open in 1871, on 27 September, was the 1½-mile-long branch from Ystrad Mynach South Junction to Penalltau Junction, thus joining the Taff Vale Extension of the Newport, Abergavenny & Hereford Railway, which ran from Pontypool Road to Aberdare; prior to this the Rhymney had obtained running powers via Hengoed West Junction to Hirwaun, which resulted in the company gaining access to the mineral wealth of the Middle Duffryn Pits, in the Aberdare area, thus providing direct competition to the Taff Vale Railway, by carrying coal to Cardiff docks. This junction at Penalltau also allowed mineral and passenger traffic to and from the Taff Bargoed branch to reach Cardiff some five years later.

On 10 January 1876 the Taff Bargoed branch, belonging jointly to the Great Western and Rhymney railways, was opened, giving access to the large ironworks and collieries of the Dowlais Iron Company, later to be known as Messrs Guest, Keen & Nettlefold, situated at Dowlais, near Merthyr Tydfil. This branch, about 9 miles in length, commenced with a junction with the

GWR at Nelson & Llancaiach, and rose continuously for a distance of 7 miles at a gradient of 1 in 40 to reach the station at Cwmbargoed, 2 miles from Dowlais and 1,250 feet above sea level. Up to 1910 the Rhymney Railway conveyed about 300,000 tons of iron-ore per year up this heavy gradient to Dowlais Ironworks; only eight or ten 10-ton wagons were capable of being drawn by one engine, making the working of the branch very laborious and expensive. It opened for passenger services on 1 February 1876, the same year that the Rhymney Railway's mineral line from Cwmbargoed station to Fochriw Colliery opened.

In 1882 another joint line with the Great Western Railway was authorised. This was the Abercanaid branch in the Taff Valley, which finally opened to traffic on 1 April 1886. It crossed the River Taff by a stone viaduct at Quakers Yard and headed towards the village of Aberfan, where a short spur re-crossed the river to reach the Merthyr Vale Colliery of Messrs Nixon. The branch then continued to Abercanaid, just north of which another viaduct took the line to the Cyfarthfa collieries and ironworks of Crawshay Brothers at Merthyr Tydfil. The Rhymney Railway joined the Hirwaun to Merthyr section of the GWR, the former Vale of Neath Railway, some 74 chains short of Merthyr High Street station – once again the Rhymney was close to Taff Vale Railway territory.

The Aber branch, for the development of the Aber Valley, located immediately north of Caerphilly, was authorised in 1890. Running from Aber Junction to the collieries at Senghenydd, this branch opened for the handling of mineral traffic and passenger services on 1 February 1894. However, some years previously, prior to the Act, a short length of track, of some 42 chains, leading from this junction to the Tregibbon Colliery, had been used for the handling of mineral traffic.

Three mineral-only lines were also opened. The Cylla branch, to develop the Cylla Valley north of Ystrad Mynach, was authorised by an Act of Parliament in 1895. This single-line branch ran from Ystrad Mynach North Junction, and was used in 1909 for the carriage of materials used in the sinking of a large colliery, later named Penalltau Colliery, for the Powell Duffryn Company; this colliery opened in 1906 and by 1910 was equipped to handle an output of a million tons of coal per year. A further 2 miles on was Penrhiwfelin Colliery; this section opened in 1909, and was closed a short time prior to the lifting of its rails in 1958. Situated about halfway along this branch was Cylla signal box, its Rhymney Railway nameplate reading 'Cylla Cabin'; this box closed in 1969, and the line to Penalltau Colliery was worked as a siding under the control of the signalman at Ystrad Mynach North signal box and the shunter. Ultimately the branch was used by 'merry-go-round' coal trains to Aberthaw Power Station, but closure came in 1991, when Penalltau Colliery was the last one producing coal in the Rhymney Valley. British Rail placed the line out of use in November 1998.

Bargoed Pits branch, a short 32-chain mineral branch, was situated 2 miles south of Bargoed station, and gave mineral traffic from Bargoed Colliery access to the main line, under the control of the Bargoed Pits signal box.

The New Tredegar Colliery branch was another short mineral branch, stretching some 60 chains to reach New Tredegar Colliery from a junction at Brithdir.

The Darran and Deri branch consisted of 2½ miles of single track, and was opened in March 1864; it was doubled in 1909. Its end-on junction with the Brecon & Merthyr Railway at Deri opened a route to the mid-Wales section of the Cambrian Railways, and thus to the Midland Railway at Tal-y-llyn and Three Cocks Junction.

In its heyday the main line and branches of the Rhymney Railway amounted to a total of 62 miles of track, with approximately 22 miles jointly owned with other railways. Today the scene has changed dramatically, with many collieries and most lines closed. The line from Ystrad Mynach North Junction to the Taff Bargoed branch via Penalltau Junction can still be seen, but it only travels as far as Cwmbargoed and the open-cast mining site there; more often than not one will see more Ministry of Defence traffic using the line rather than coal trains. The Bute West and East Docks at Cardiff are no more, replaced by the Cardiff Bay development; the very few warehouses that survived were quickly converted into rather expensive flats. The original main line, which became the Walnut Tree branch, is now a pleasant cycle track and walk, part of the Taff Trail, while the Caerphilly branch has reverted to nature, except for the area near Penrhos Junction, which is now filled in and part of a new housing estate. The Abercanaid branch has been obliterated by the extension of the new A470 trunk road, which follows the River Taff, much as the Rhymney Railway did in better days.

The Aber branch has also mostly gone. Aber Junction is now a factory site and wagon park, and Abertridwr station and the nearby colliery site are now landscaped and built upon. The Cylla branch has had its tracks lifted, although the sleepers have been left, with buddleia – the favourite bush of butterflies and railways – growing in abundance. The Darran and Deri branch has also become a cycle track, part of the Northern Rhymney Valley countryside service; a short distance along the line, at Deri, can be seen the remains of a rather unusual Grade 3 listed bridge (see page 41); however, its condition is deteriorating, and I feel that it is one thing to preserve a structure, but perhaps such orders should include protection as well.

Above **'5700' Class 0-6-0PT No 7724 approaches Llanbradach Colliery with a Coke Ovens to Pontypool Road freight on 27 April 1957. Llanbradach station and signal box can be seen in the distance. This locomotive was built in 1930 by Kerr Stuart & Co, works number 4459, and was withdrawn in 1962.** *B. J. Miller collection*

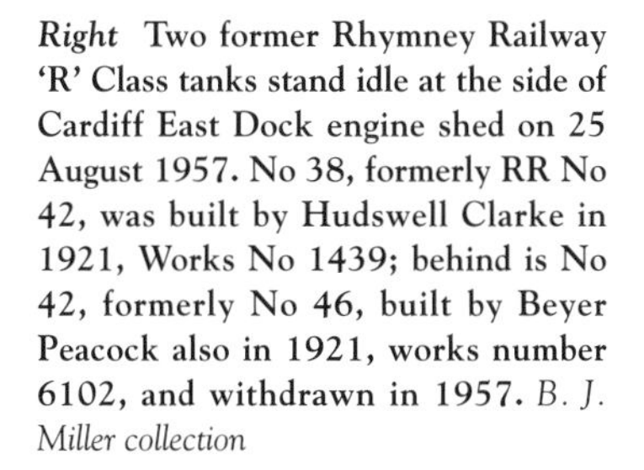

Right **Two former Rhymney Railway 'R' Class tanks stand idle at the side of Cardiff East Dock engine shed on 25 August 1957. No 38, formerly RR No 42, was built by Hudswell Clarke in 1921, Works No 1439; behind is No 42, formerly No 46, built by Beyer Peacock also in 1921, works number 6102, and withdrawn in 1957.** *B. J. Miller collection*

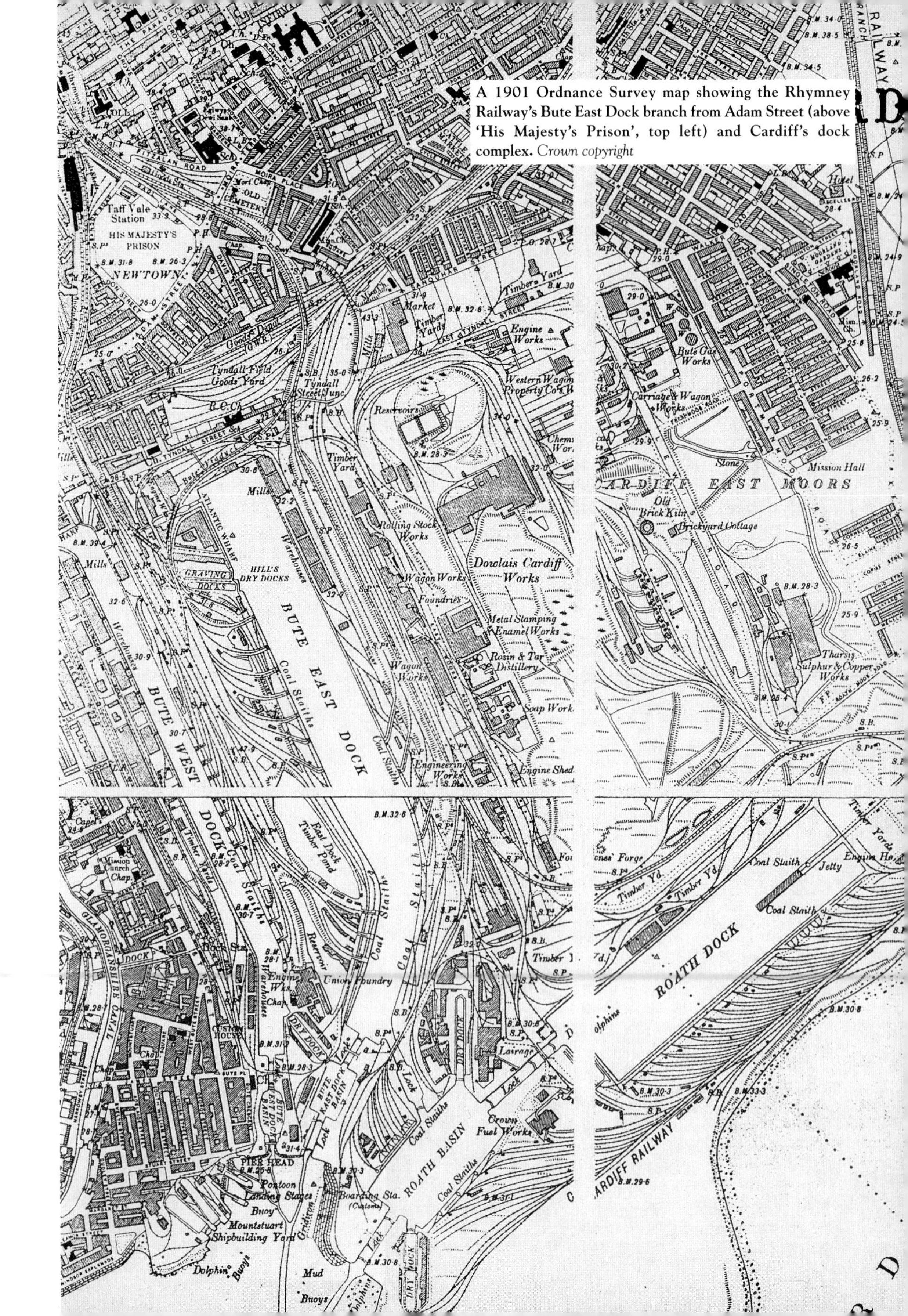

A 1901 Ordnance Survey map showing the Rhymney Railway's Bute East Dock branch from Adam Street (above 'His Majesty's Prison', top left) and Cardiff's dock complex. *Crown copyright*

1. BUTE EAST DOCK BRANCH

The Bute East Dock branch in Cardiff opened in September 1857. By 1880 the amount of coal and coke traffic it carried reached 960,000 tons, in 1887 the total was 1,470,000 tons, in 1890 1,895,000 tons, and more than 3,000,000 tons by 1910. This traffic was taken direct by Rhymney Railway engines over the dock railway network, which belonged to the Bute Docks Company (later becoming the Cardiff Railway Company), and on to the sidings leading to the tips, where the coal was then handled by employees of the docks company and tipped into the waiting vessels.

In 1910 the Rhymney Railway was also handing over to the Taff Vale Railway at Penarth Junction, near Radyr, a total of three-quarters of a million tons of traffic per year, and to the Barry Railway at Penrhos Junction a total of one and a half million tons per year, for shipment from Barry Docks. In addition to the coal and coke traffic carried at this time, the Rhymney Railway also conveyed about 5,000,000 tons of iron and iron ore from Cardiff Docks to the Dowlais and Cyfarthfa Works.

Also in that year large quantities of pitwood for use in the collieries had to be transported from the docks, in addition to general merchandise, making the average annual total tonnage carried over the Rhymney Railway system more than 9,000,000 tons per year.

At the inland end of the branch was Cardiff Adam Street station, which opened on 31 March 1858. It closed to passenger services on 1 April 1871 (passenger services were transferred to the Rhymney Railway's new Parade station, opened the same day). Adam Street station remained open for the handling of goods traffic until closure on 2 May 1966.

The opening of the new passenger station at Adam Street in Cardiff brought a flurry of excitement to the people of the town, and the *Cardiff & Merthyr Guardian*'s edition of Saturday 3 April 1858 celebrated the achievement:

CARDIFF AND RHYMNEY RAILWAY

The Cardiff and Rhymney Railway was opened on Wednesday last for goods and passenger traffic, and we congratulate our friends in Rhymney and in Cardiff that a direct communication by rail is accomplished, the forerunner of great mining activity along this line, cheaper tolls from Rhymney, and a large increase to the shipping business of Cardiff.

The passenger station of this railway is now in course of erection at the Cemetery Bridge, Adam Street, the most central point that could be selected, and for passengers going to and from the South Wales Railway, the distance to be traversed is almost in a direct line. It is along one continuous main thoroughfare presenting not the slightest difficulty to the stranger.

CHEAP TRAINS FOR EASTER

A new country has been opened to the excursion by the Cardiff and Rhymney Railway, which commenced running passenger trains on Wednesday last. This company has commenced in right good earnest to give those 'in search of the picturesque' the full benefit of cheap fares. This day [Good Friday] return tickets have been issued at a fare and a half, available until next Tuesday evening. On Sunday return tickets will be issued at one fare, on the Monday and Tuesday return tickets will be issued to Caerphilly, so celebrated for its carefully preserved ruin of its ancient castle, at a fare and a half, those issued on Monday being available until next evening' On Thursday and Friday tickets will be issued at single fares for the double journey to Abergavenny races. For detailed particulars, see advertisement. [Reproduced on page 13]

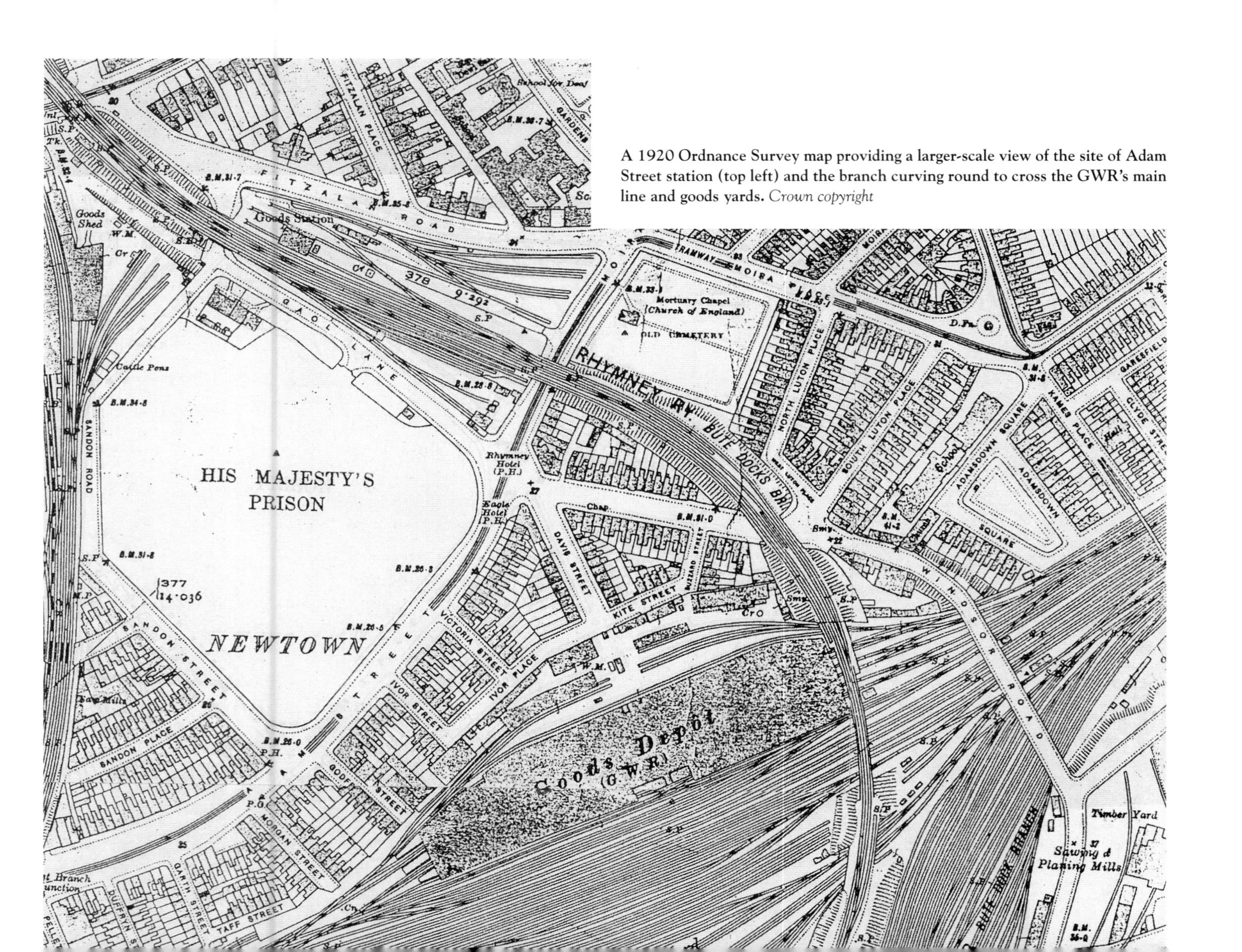

A 1920 Ordnance Survey map providing a larger-scale view of the site of Adam Street station (top left) and the branch curving round to cross the GWR's main line and goods yards. *Crown copyright*

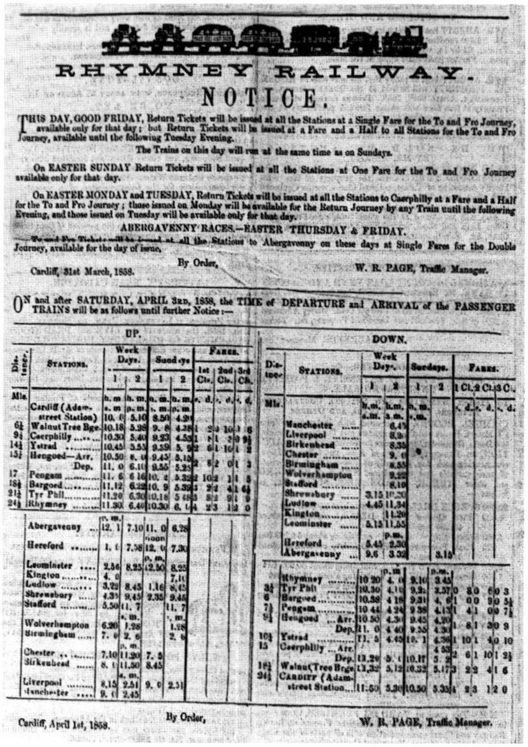

RHYMNEY RAILWAY.

NOTICE.

THIS DAY, GOOD FRIDAY, Return Tickets will be issued at all the Stations at a Single Fare for the To and Fro Journey, available only for that day; but Return Tickets will be issued at a Fare and a Half to all Stations for the To and Fro Journey, available until the following Tuesday Evening.

The Trains on this day will run at the same time as on Sundays.

On EASTER SUNDAY Return Tickets will be issued at all the Stations at One Fare for the To and Fro Journey available only for that day.

On EASTER MONDAY and TUESDAY, Return Tickets will be issued at all the Stations to Caerphilly at a Fare and a Half for the To and Fro Journey; those issued on Monday will be available for the Return Journey by any Train until the following Evening, and those issued on Tuesday will be available only for that day.

ABERGAVENNY RACES.—EASTER THURSDAY & FRIDAY.

To and Fro Tickets will be issued at all the Stations to Abergavenny on these days at Single Fares for the Double Journey, available for the day of issue.

Cardiff, 31st March, 1858. By Order, W. R. PAGE, Traffic Manager.

ON and after SATURDAY, APRIL 3RD, 1858, the TIME of DEPARTURE and ARRIVAL of the PASSENGER TRAINS will be as follows until further Notice:—

UP.

Distance	Stations	Week Days 1	Week Days 2	Sundays 1	Sundays 2	Fares 1st Cl.	Fares 2nd Cl.	Fares 3rd Cl.
Mls.		h. m. a. m.	h. m. p. m.	h. m. a. m.	h. m. p. m.	s. d.	s. d.	s. d.
	Cardiff (Adam-street Station)	10. 0	5.10	8.50	4.20			
6½	Walnut Tree Bge.	10.18	5.28	9. 8	4.38	1 2	10	6
9½	Caerphilly	10.30	5.40	9.23	4.53	1 [illegible]	1 2	9½
14½	Ystrad	10.45	5.53	9.39	5. 9	2 6	1 10	1 2
15½	Hengoed—Arr.	10.50	6. 0	9.45	5.15			
	Dep.	11. 0	6.10	9.55	5.25	2 8	2 0	1 3
17	Pengam	11. 6	6.16	10. 2	5.32	2 10	2 1	1 5
18¾	Bargoed	11.12	6.22	10. 9	5.39	3 2	2 4	1 6½
21½	Tyr Phil	11.20	6.30	10.18	5.48	3 8	2 9	1 9
24½	Rhymney	11.30	6.40	10.30	6. 0	4 2	3 1	2 0
	Abergavenny	p. m. 12. 1	7.10	11. 0	6.28			
	Hereford	1. 0	7.58	noon 12. 0	7.30			
	Leominster	2.36	8.25	p. m. 12.50	8.25			
	Kington	4. 0			7.10			
	Ludlow	3.22	8.45	1.16	8.45			
	Shrewsbury	4.35	9.45	2.35	9.45			
	Stafford	5.50	11. 7		11. 7			
	Wolverhampton	6.20	a. m. 1.28		a. m. 1.28			
	Birmingham	7. 0	2. 6		2. 6			
	Chester	7.10	p. m. 11.20	7. 5				
	Birkenhead	8. 0	11.50	8.45				
	Liverpool	8.15	a. m. 2.51	9. 0	2.31			
	Manchester	9. 0	2.45					

DOWN.

Distance	Stations	Week Days 1	Week Days 2	Sundays 1	Sundays 2	Fares 1 Cl.	Fares 2 Cl.	Fares 3 Cl.
Mls.		h. m. a. m.	h. m. a. m.	h. m. a. m.		s. d.	s. d.	s. d.
	Manchester		6.45					
	Liverpool		8.20					
	Birkenhead		8.35					
	Chester		9. 0					
	Birmingham		8.55					
	Wolverhampton		9.22					
	Stafford		8.16					
	Shrewsbury	3.15	10.20					
	Ludlow	4.45	11.34					
	Kington		11.20					
	Leominster	5.15	11.55					
	Hereford	5.45	p.m. 2.30					
	Abergavenny	9.6	3.32		3.15			
	Rhymney	10 20	p. m. 4. 0	9.10	p. m. 3.45			
3½	Tyr Phil	10.30	4.10	9.2[illegible]	3.57	0 8	0 6	0 3
6	Bargoed	10.38	4.18	9.31	4. 6	1 0	0 9	0 5½
7½	Pengam	10 44	4.24	9.38	4.13	1 4	1 0	0 7½
9¾	Hengoed ... Arr.	10.50	4.30	9.45	4.20			
	Dep.	11. 0	4.40	9.55	4.30	1 8	1 3	0 9
10¾	Ystrad	11. 5	4.45	10. 1	4.36	1 10	1 4	0 10
15	Caerphilly ... Arr.				4.53			
	Dep.	11.20	5. 0	10.17	5. 2	2 6	1 10	1 2½
18½	Walnut Tree Brge	11.32	5.12	10.32	5.17	3 2	2 4	1 6
24½	CARDIFF (Adam-street Station)	11.50	5.30	10.50	5.33	4 2	3 1	2 0

Cardiff, April 1st, 1858. By Order, W. R. PAGE, Traffic Manager.

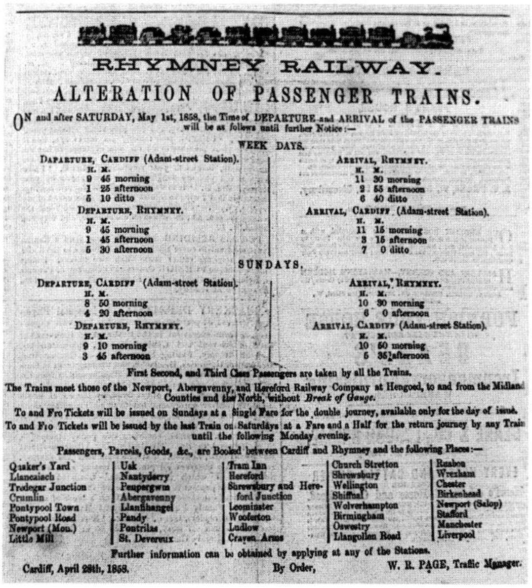

RHYMNEY RAILWAY.

ALTERATION OF PASSENGER TRAINS.

ON and after SATURDAY, May 1st, 1858, the Time of DEPARTURE and ARRIVAL of the PASSENGER TRAINS will be as follows until further Notice:—

WEEK DAYS.

Departure, Cardiff (Adam-street Station).	Arrival, Rhymney.
H. M.	H. M.
9 45 morning	11 30 morning
1 25 afternoon	2 55 afternoon
5 10 ditto	6 40 ditto

Departure, Rhymney.	Arrival, Cardiff (Adam-street Station).
H. M.	H. M.
9 45 morning	11 15 morning
1 45 afternoon	3 15 afternoon
5 30 afternoon	7 0 ditto

SUNDAYS.

Departure, Cardiff (Adam-street Station).	Arrival, Rhymney.
H. M.	H. M.
8 50 morning	10 30 morning
4 20 afternoon	6 0 afternoon

Departure, Rhymney.	Arrival, Cardiff (Adam-street Station).
H. M.	H. M.
9 10 morning	10 50 morning
3 45 afternoon	5 35 afternoon

First Second, and Third Class Passengers are taken by all the Trains.

The Trains meet those of the Newport, Abergavenny, and Hereford Railway Company at Hengoed, to and from the Midland Counties and the North, without *Break of Gauge.*

To and Fro Tickets will be issued on Sundays at a Single Fare for the double journey, available only for the day of issue.

To and Fro Tickets will be issued by the last Train on Saturdays at a Fare and a Half for the return journey by any Train until the following Monday evening.

Passengers, Parcels, Goods, &c., are Booked between Cardiff and Rhymney and the following Places:—

Quaker's Yard	Usk	Tram Inn	Church Stretton	Ruabon
Llancaiach	Nantyderry	Hereford	Shrewsbury	Wrexham
Tredegar Junction	Penpergwm	Shrewsbury and Hereford Junction	Wellington	Chester
Crumlin	Abergavenny	Leominster	Shiffnal	Birkenhead
Pontypool Town	Llanfihangel	Woofferton	Wolverhampton	Newport (Salop)
Pontypool Road	Pandy	Ludlow	Birmingham	Stafford
Newport (Mon.)	Pontrilas	Craven Arms	Oswestry	Manchester
Little Mill	St. Devereux		Llangollen Road	Liverpool

Further information can be obtained by applying at any of the Stations.

Cardiff, April 28th, 1858. By Order, W. R. PAGE, Traffic Manager.

Left A notice in the *Cardiff & Merthyr Guardian* of Saturday 3 April 1858, announcing the first day of services, not only for the Rhymney Valley, but also for connections to the town of Abergavenny – a special passenger train would be running to the races there, and to the Midlands. *South Glamorgan Libraries*

Above Another Rhymney Railway notice in the 1 May 1858 edition of the paper. *South Glamorgan Libraries*

On Saturday 30 January 1858 the *Cardiff & Merthyr Guardian* reported to its readers:

THE OPENING OF THE EXTENSION OF THE EAST BUTE DOCK

In our impressions of last week, we briefly alluded to this event. We are now enabled to give additional particulars, chiefly as to the prospective advantages likely to result to the trade of the Port of Cardiff. On Tuesday the 19th inst, Mr Boyle, the acting trustee of the Marquis of Bute, accompanied by Lieutenant Dornford, the dock master, Mr Clarke, mining engineer, Mr Macconnochi, the resident dock engineer (acting for Messrs Walter, Burgess, and Cooper), Messrs Hemingways and Pearson, the dock contractors, Mr Smithson and Mr Page, the chief officials of the Rhymney Railway, made a formal opening of this important sheet of water, by towing the beautiful barque, the 'Cornelia of Leith', of about 700 tons register, from that portion of the East Dock, which has been in use about two and a half years, into the extension dock.

Our readers will be interested to learn that this extension is in extent 20 acres, with a depth of water of 25 feet and width of 500 feet. This auxiliary dock accommodation must be regarded as of great importance for the Port of Cardiff, and will not fail to aid materially the development of the mineral resources of the eastern and most valuable portion of the South Wales mineral basin, by its affording the means of shipment of a large quantity of produce.

The dock does not, of course, meet all the requirements of a heavy mineral and iron traffic – a great deal more is required, and considerable works have been, and are being made for giving adequate facilities for the shipment of goods.

At the present time there are three coal staiths on the western side of East Dock, approached from the Taff Vale Railway, and on the eastern side there are four staiths belonging to the Rhymney Railway Company. The latter are nearly ready to be

> used, and in addition the trustees are erecting five staiths on the western side, making a total of twelve staiths on the East Dock. Of this number, three are in working order, four will be ready in a very short time, and the remaining five in about three months, the whole representing a coal traffic of one million tons, to which may be added the Rhymney Iron Company's traffic of, say, 100,000 tons, and taking the traffic from other sources at 100,000 tons, we have an aggregate traffic for the East Dock of 1,200,000 tons. If we take the exports and imports of Cardiff in the year 1857, in round numbers, at two million tons, we can properly estimate the extent of this additional dock accommodation, which as the figures indicate, exceeds one half of the present trade of the port.
>
> Be it understood that this is not the maximum trade which may be done. A large quay or water frontage remains unoccupied, on which six staiths may be conveniently erected, which six staiths would afford a proportionate rate of shipment. Moreover the trustees, believing in the generally received opinion of the valuable resources of the district through which the Taff Vale and other railways, having their termini at Cardiff, traverse, have not hesitated to afford a further extension of the Bute Dock, which is now in progress, and which will most probably be completed this year. This further extension will be fifteen acres, making the whole representing, when completed, shipping accommodation equal to the entire trade of Cardiff at the present time, and forming, perhaps, the largest sheet of water enclosed as a dock, for shipping of heavy tonnage in the kingdom. Consequently, upon so large an export trade, the trustees contemplate making suitable provision for an export trade, and are prepared to appropriate a large portion of the north end of East Dock for public quays and warehouses, with suitable roads and railways, by which the greatest facilities will be given to the trade of the town, and the districts having communication by means of the railways.

Bute East Basin and the first part of East Dock opened in 1855, followed by the East Dock Extension in 1858, and the last part of the Bute East Dock in 1859.

In 1922 the privately owned dock companies of South Wales, which included the Cardiff Docks network, were amalgamated with other ports to become part of the docks department of the Great Western Railway.

With the decline in coal and steel production as collieries and steel works were closed and alternative sources found, Bute East Dock was closed to coal and other exports in 1970. In 1988 the docks began a period of massive change: the East Dock became an enclosed marina as part of the Cardiff Bay project, and the West Dock was filled in and built upon. Today all traffic, both export and import, uses the Queen Alexandra Dock or the Roath Dock, such trade consisting of the export of scrap metal and steel, and the import of timber, non-ferrous metals, rubber, tin and fruit.

Robert Stephenson, the talented son of George, was involved with the development of the Bute Docks as engineer and architect: the entrance to the Bute Docks ship canal in 1840, the Bute Dock Basin, and Bute West Dock with its wharfs and the land development around it. While involved with these plans Stephenson had thoughts for a new type of coal tip, and on 8 February 1847 he completed his drawings for a structure whereby a fully loaded coal wagon would be held in place above the vessel, then tilted to allow the coal to slide down into the ship's hold. It was a work of pure genius. It was no surprise, therefore, that from 1851 to the opening of the Bute East Dock Stephenson was to act as arbitrator to settle any differences or problems that arose.

20° & 21° VICTORIÆ, *Cap.* cxl.

Rhymney Railway Act, 1857.

SCHEDULE to which the foregoing Act refers.

MEMORANDUM OF AGREEMENT dated this Thirty-first Day of March One thousand eight hundred and fifty-one.

IT is agreed between the South Wales Railway Company of the First Part, and the Right Honourable Lord James Stuart, Onesiphorus Tyndall Bruce, and James Munro Macnabb, as Representatives of the late Marquis of Bute, of the Second Part, as follows:

First. The South Wales Railway Company shall abandon the Branch Railways proposed in their Bill now before Parliament to the Glamorganshire Canal and the Bute Dock.

Second. In consideration of such Abandonment, the Parties hereto of the Second Part undertake to expend a Sum of Money not exceeding One hundred and eighty thousand Pounds in the Execution of Works for a new Dock or Basin at Cardiff to the East of the existing Docks, with a new Entrance to the present Cut (unless Mr. Robert Stephenson shall be of opinion that such new Entrance is unnecessary), with all proper and usual Quays, Landing Places, and other Works and Conveniences connected therewith, such Dock to be constructed of a greater Depth than the present Dock, according to a Plan to be agreed upon between the Parties, and in case of Difference between them according to a Plan to be prepared by Mr. Robert Stephenson as Arbitrator acting indifferently between the Parties.

Third. That such Dock and other Works shall be proceeded with with all reasonable Despatch, and so at least to permit of its being opened and Accommodation afforded for shipping Goods and Minerals therein on or before the First Day of September One thousand eight hundred and fifty-three.

Fourth. The South Wales Railway Company to apply if necessary to Parliament in the next Session for Power to construct a Branch Railway to and along the East Side of the said proposed Dock, according to a Plan and Section to be determined on by the Engineer of that Company, and to construct such Branch Railway so as that it shall be opened on or before the First September One thousand eight hundred and fifty-three; and the Parties hereto of the Second Part, in consideration of the Trade which will be brought to the said Dock by means of such Branch, to grant a Lease for Two hundred and fifty Years of the Land necessary for the Construction of such Branch, the Rent to be estimated upon a fair and reasonable Valuation of the present Value of the Land, without reference to the proposed new Dock, and to be converted into a Tonnage Rate upon the Articles conveyed thereon, such Rent to be so ascertained and determined by Mr. Robert Stephenson.

Fifth.

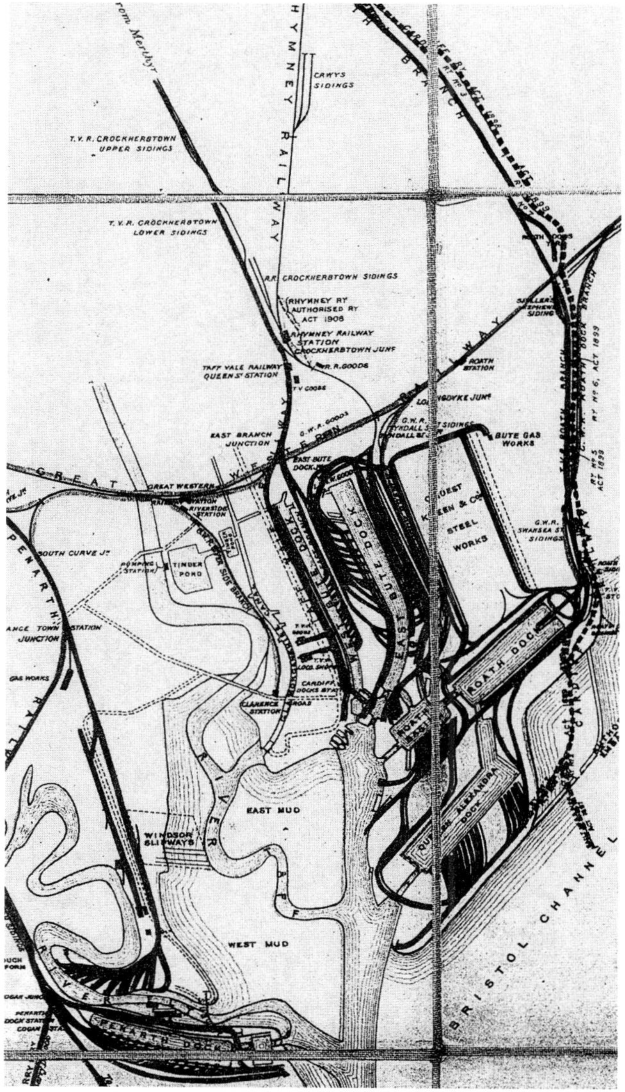

Far left **Schedule dated 31 March 1851, from the Act of Parliament of 1857, showing Robert Stephenson's role as arbitrator in the development of the docks.** *Author's collection*

Left **Cardiff's docks and the railway companies serving them, from a Taff Vale Railway District Map of 1910.** *A. Powell*

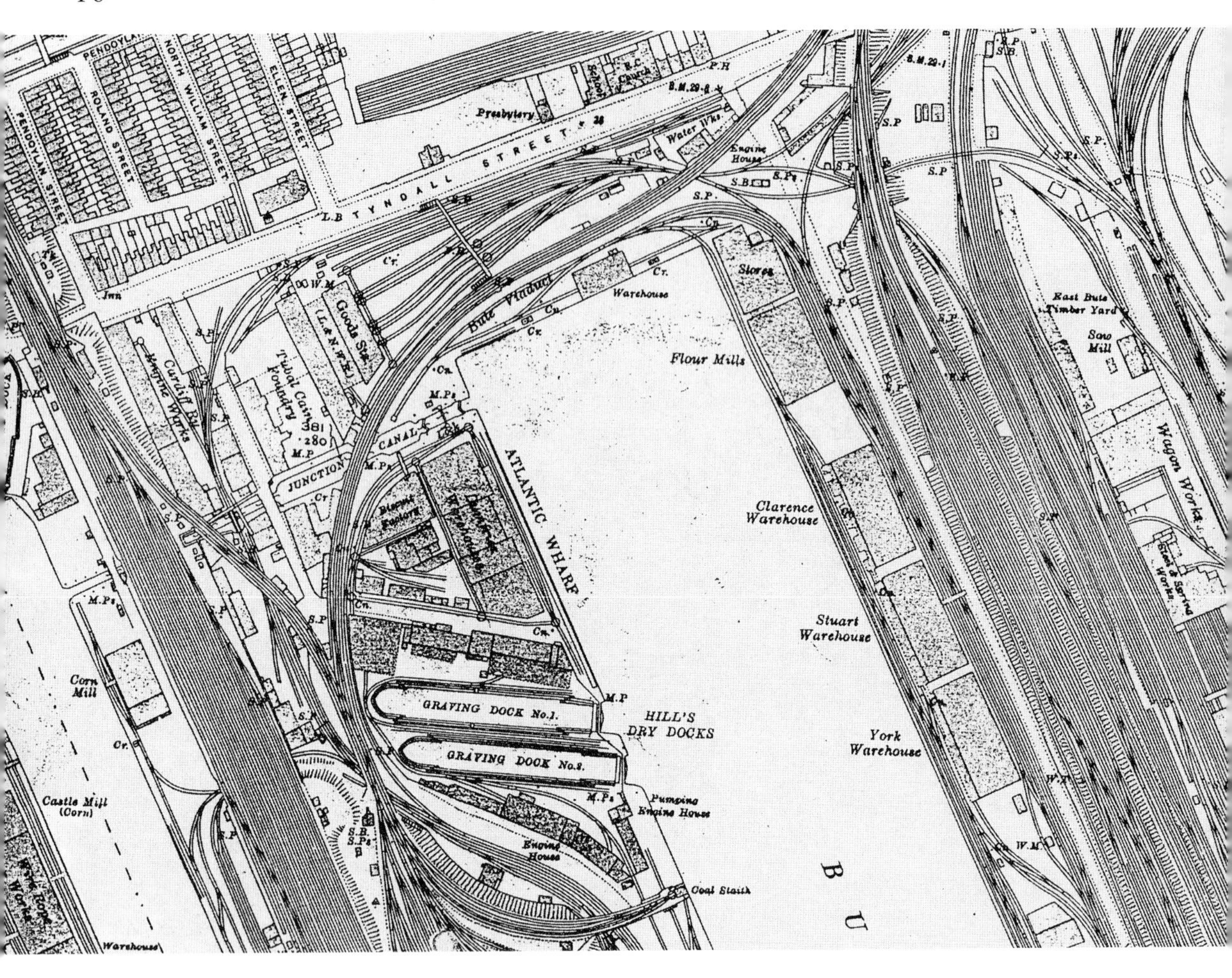

Above **An Ordnance Survey map 1920 showing the north end of Bute East Dock.** *Crown Copyright*

Below left An aerial view of Bute West Dock (left) and East Dock (right), looking north. At the top right-hand corner, leading to the centre area of the two docks, is the embankment and viaduct that carried the Rhymney lines to the coal staiths on the west side of East Dock. In the top left-hand corner is the Glamorganshire Canal, while on the east side of West Dock are the former TVR lines, en route to their staiths. At the bottom right-hand are the staiths used for handling coal from the Rhymney Railway, while the other staiths can be seen clearly on the west side of the dock. In the north-west area of East Dock can be seen the Graving Dock. The vessels in the centre of East Dock are laid up, waiting for cargoes and with their crews paid off; this photograph was taken on 6 August 1930, when work was scarce and the Depression was cutting deep, especially in the coal-mining areas and docks of South Wales and the North East of England. *Associated British Ports*

Above Another aerial view of the docks, this time looking south. In the bottom right-hand corner is the Rhymney Railway line leading to Bute East Dock, after crossing the main GWR South Wales line that ran in front of the GWR's Tyndall Street Goods Depot (see the map on page 12), and on to the embankment taking it in front of the East Dock and round to the west side. On the east side, in the centre of the photograph, the vessel at berth is at the timber quay. Opposite this ship, on the west side of the dock, are two vessels at the coaling staiths; the roads leading to them can be seen quite clearly. The vessel at the extreme right is berthed at the Atlantic Wharf. At the far end of the dock is the lock leading into Roath Basin, connected with which, on the left, is Roath Dock. At the southern tip of the East and West Docks, between their basins, can be seen a solitary building with a tall tower; this is the Pierhead building, headquarters of the Cardiff Railway Company (formerly the Bute Docks Company), and until very recently the headquarters of Associated British Ports. *Rhondda Borough Libraries*

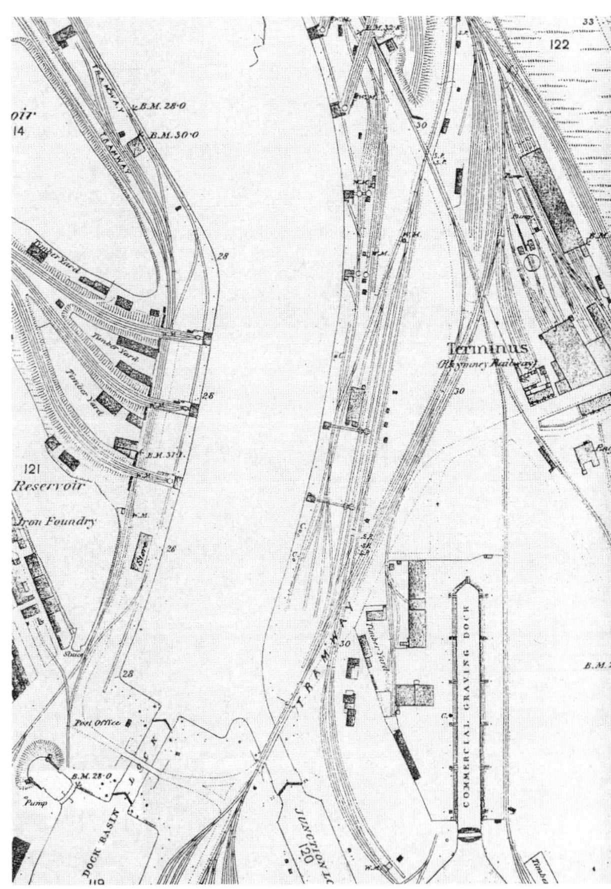

Above Part of an 1882 Ordnance Survey map of the south end of Bute East Dock, showing the Rhymney Railway's goods terminus (top right) and the lock leading out into East Dock Basin and Roath Basin (bottom left). *Crown copyright*

Top No 2 coal tip, on the west side of East Dock, photographed from on board a vessel at anchor in the dock, at 3pm on 22 April 1884. *Associated British Ports*

Middle and bottom Two tips on the east side of Bute East Dock, photographed respectively at 11.30am on 23 April and 10.45am on 26 April 1884, the latter being the GWR's No 1 tip. *Associated British Ports*

Top The west side of Bute East Dock, c1906, showing the preparation of the new approach roads to the coaling hoists. Most of the wagons in view are Great Western Railway open plank wagons, with one Great Eastern and a few private owner colliery wagons, from Llanbradach and Cribbwr Fawr; the latter little-known colliery produced household and manufacturing coal, and supplied the Port Talbot and Swansea area. *Associated British Ports*

Middle On an unknown date, new roads to the coal staiths are in process of construction. The concrete retaining wall is complete and wagons are bringing spoil to build up the banks. Wooden planks, possibly shoring timbers, can be seen lying around ready for use by the contractors at a later date, and a hive of activity can be seen at the lineside. *Associated British Ports*

Bottom This photograph shows just how busy the East Dock was in 1906, with discharging of cargo from ship direct to warehouse. These 30-ton movable cranes had a luffing jib with either a 3-ton or 6-ton lift, but it is difficult to guess what cargo is in the buckets. These warehouses, in the north-eastern corner of the dock, were named York (nearest camera), Stuart and Clarence (see the map on page 16); the building in the distance, with the clock tower, is a flour mill. The open plank wagons in view nearest the camera are all empty and may have been carrying the wooden planks seen on the right in rather untidy stacks. *Associated British Ports*

Above Another view of the warehouses in the north-east corner of Bute East Dock, which bags of Canadian sugar being discharged from the SS *Hillglade* in August 1927. The flour mill with its clock tower can be seen more clearly. Note the newer movable cranes, quite different from the older luffing cranes. Judging by the amount of activity, it looks as though these three warehouses are still just as busy as they had been 20 years earlier. *Associated British Ports*

Below Looking from York warehouse south towards the new Timber Quay at the east side of East Dock, ready for use on Monday 12 June 1939. SS *Merkur*, SS *Storsjeld*, SS *Kelvaldis*, SS *Skrun* and SS *Runa* are at their berths after discharging their timber cargoes into waiting railway wagons. At the bottom right of the photograph can be seen a private owner wagon from the Ocean Colliery, Treorchy; this wagon carried a 10-ton load, and had a livery consisting of a black body with white lettering. *Associated British Ports*

Above The heroic actions of dockers and railwaymen on the night of 3/4 March 1941 should be remembered, as these docks (as well as others in South Wales) went up in flames. That night German bombers dropped their deadly loads of high-explosive and incendiary bombs time and time again, and fires raged as warehouses, factories, timber stocks and ships caught the full blast of these deadly weapons. This is the west side of East Dock, near No 7 coal hoist, showing the damage caused by German high-explosive bombs to the roadway, permanent way and wagon-repairing premises. *Associated British Ports*

Below A Luftwaffe bombing map, dated June 1941, issued to the crews of German bombers to guide them on to targets in and around Cardiff. *Mid Glamorgan Libraries*

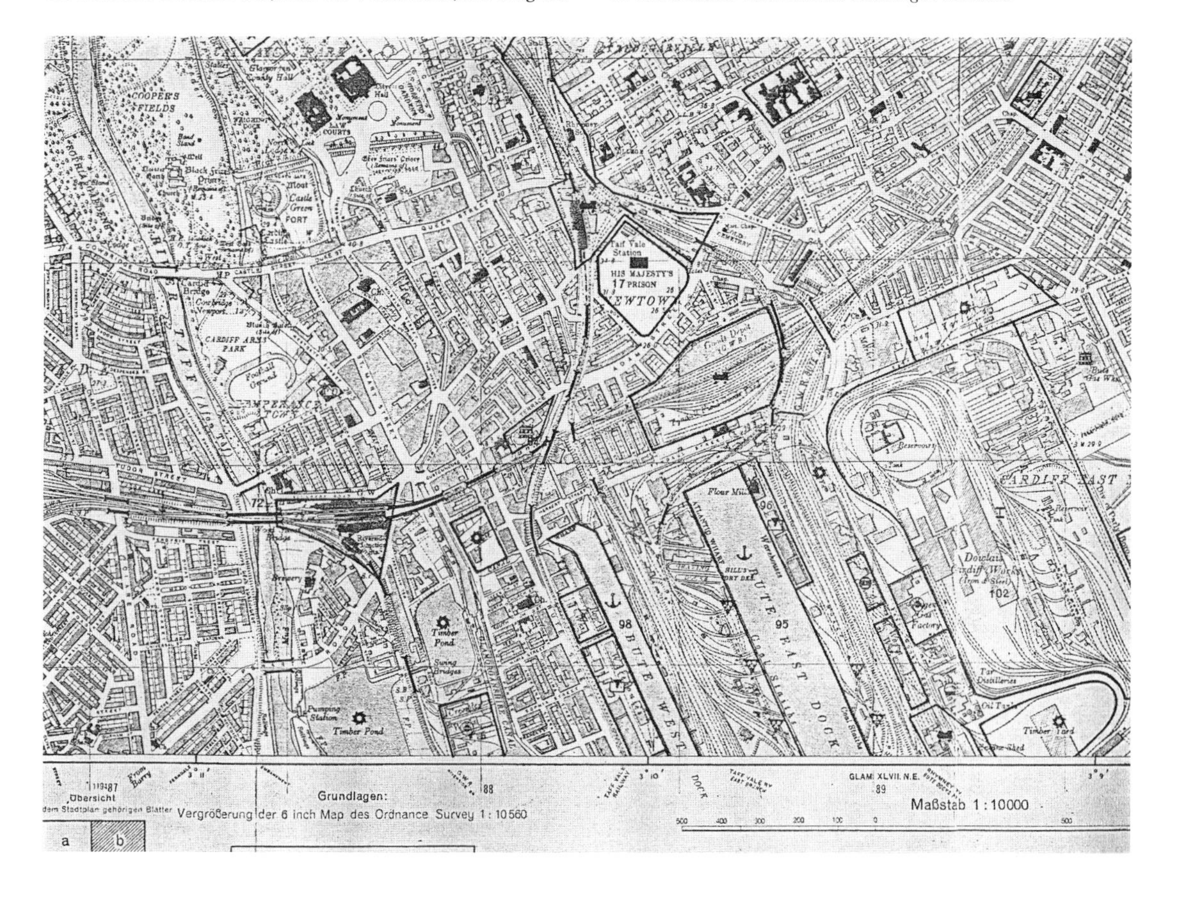

Discharging Finnish pit-props from ship to GWR open wagons at East Dock on 6 November 1945. From right to left the wagon numbers read 2047 (four-plank), 202820 (five-plank) and 203669 (four-plank); stencilled on in white paint are the words 'For use at Cardiff Docks only.' *Associated British Ports*

Ingot mouldings at Cardiff Docks en route to the USA in about 1962. They have come down from the Dowlais Works on this rather unusual 'Flatrol' low-loader, No 32905. *The late John A. Owen collection*

Above This Rhymney Railway 'K' Class saddle tank was photographed running light in Cardiff Docks on 11 August 1924. *LCGB, Ken Nunn Collection*

Below No 48 is another Rhymney Railway saddle tank. Built in 1884 by Sharp Stewart & Co, works number 3177, it was re-numbered 612 by the GWR, and withdrawn between 1925 and 1927. It is seen on 25 April 1910 outside the Rhymney engine shed, which was opened in 1857 and closed on 19 January 1931, only to be replaced by a GWR-built engine shed that same year. *LCGB, Ken Nunn Collection*

Above Engine No 55 stands at Cardiff East Dock engine shed on 1 May 1927. Originally Rhymney Railway 'A' Class No 13, it was built by the firm of Robert Stephenson & Co, works number 3390, in May 1910. Rebuilt by the GWR in November 1929, it was withdrawn from service in February 1953. *F. T. Hornby collection*

Below In this second view of the engine shed at East Dock, on the left is a Rhymney Railway 'R' Class engine with its GWR number 37; this engine was built at the Hudswell Clarke works in 1921, works number 1438, and later, in GWR service, was rebuilt with a parallel boiler. Formerly Rhymney Railway No 41, it was withdrawn from service in September 1956. On the right is a former Taff Vale Railway engine with its GWR number 371. An 'A' Class engine, built by Nasmyth Wilson, works number 1271, in 1919, it was TVR No 136. The engine shed is the GWR rebuild of 1931; it closed in March 1958, then re-opened in September 1962 for the servicing of steam engines after Canton engine shed closed, eventually being reconstructed into a diesel servicing depot. *The late N. L. Browne, courtesy of Mr F. T. Hornby*

2. WALNUT TREE BRANCH

What became known as the Walnut Tree branch was originally the main line to Cardiff from the Rhymney Valley for minerals and passenger traffic. The line was opened for mineral and freight traffic on 25 February 1858, and to passenger services on 31 March. It lost its passenger services when the new main line direct from Caerphilly to Cardiff was opened with the completion of Cefn On Tunnel at Caerphilly.

Shortly after the opening of the passenger services to Rhymney, the *Cardiff & Merthyr Guardian* sent a reporter to describe this new mode of travel, and on Saturday 8 May 1858 the following article appeared:

A TRIP FROM CARDIFF TO RHYMNEY

Having taken our tickets at Adam Street Station, and seated ourselves in one of the carriages, the train presently started at a slow but safe pace along the Taff Vale Railway through a country which is so well known to the majority of our readers that it needs no description.

In the short space of 25 minutes we reached Pentyrch Bridge, which crosses the Taff, and in a few seconds after we halted at Walnut Tree Bridge Station, where the Rhymney line diverges from the Taff Vale, in a north-easterly direction, under the steep hill of Craig-yr-Alt, just above Nantgarw. From this point is an extensive view of the Vale of the Taff, Treforest works, and Newbridge being seen in the distance. At this place the line turns to the east through the deep cutting of Pentyrebeg, the slips and incidents of which we have so often noticed during its formation. Just as we emerge from this entrenchment, Caerphilly Castle comes into sight, the majestic grandeur of which strikes the beholder with awe and admiration. Passing Cwrtdrawlyn and Beddau farms we arrive at Caerphilly Station.

To the east from here are seen the gently sloping meadows and fields in the parish of Bedwas, the high cultivation of which adds so much to the beauty of the scenery in this delightful neighbourhood. Fields which were thirty years ago full of brambles and furze are now in a state of the highest cultivation, even to the verge of Mynydd-y-Grug and Mynydd-y-Dimlith.

In the summer season the spectator may see several sets of reapers gathering the rich bounties of Ceres, on the various farms in this locality, as the farmers here vie with each other in reaping for the earliest, the land lying in a kind of extensive amphitheatre so

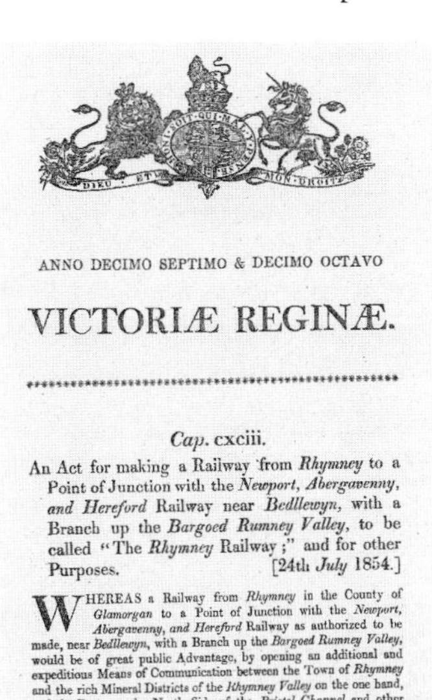

ANNO DECIMO SEPTIMO & DECIMO OCTAVO

VICTORIÆ REGINÆ.

Cap. cxciii.

An Act for making a Railway from *Rhymney* to a Point of Junction with the *Newport, Abergavenny, and Hereford* Railway near *Bedllewyn*, with a Branch up the *Bargoed Rumney Valley*, to be called "The *Rhymney* Railway;" and for other Purposes. [24th *July* 1854.]

WHEREAS a Railway from *Rhymney* in the County of *Glamorgan* to a Point of Junction with the *Newport, Abergavenny, and Hereford* Railway as authorized to be made, near *Bedllewyn*, with a Branch up the *Bargoed Rumney Valley*, would be of great public Advantage, by opening an additional and expeditious Means of Communication between the Town of *Rhymney* and the rich Mineral Districts of the *Rhymney Valley* on the one hand, and the Ports on the North Side of the *Bristol Channel* and other Places on the other hand: And whereas the Persons herein-after named are willing, at their own Expense, to carry the said Undertaking into effect: And whereas the Objects aforesaid cannot be effected without the Authority of Parliament: May it therefore please Your Majesty that it may be enacted; and be it enacted by the Queen's most Excellent Majesty, by and with the Advice and Consent of the

[*Local.*] 36 *X* Lords

The first page of the Act of Parliament, passed by the House of Lords on 24 July 1854, the first step in the making of the Rhymney Railway. *Author's collection*

Lan
Spring
Cwm-Dylluan
Old Quarries
Craig y Lan
Old Quarry
Tyn-y-daren
Coal Level
Quarry
Gwaelod-y-garth
Old Quarries
Capel Salem
Shaft
Hotel
Old Coal Level
Taffswell
Tir-ffynnon Daf
School
Gas Works
Capel Bethlehem
Old Shaft
Old Tramway
Old Air Shaft
Old Coal Level
Maesaraul
Coed Rhiw-ceiliog
Maes-gwyn
Quarry
Glamorgan Brick Works
Tyn-y-coed
Georgetown
Penlyrch Iron Works (Disused)
Tynewydd
Old Trial Shaft
Old Tramway
Old Ironstone Level
Old Quarry
Trough
Nant Cwm-llwydrew
Garth Wood
Old Shaft
Old Air Shaft
Mine Pit Cottage
Old Quarries
Ton-mawr
Chwarre Glâs (Disused)
Old Coal Level
Penlyrch Steel & Tin Plate Works
Twyn'r aderyn
River Taff (Afon Taf)
TAFF VALE RAILWAY
Locks
Station
Glan-y-llyn
Church Hall
Bryn-côch Colliery (Disused)
Reservoir
Rockwood Colliery
Slant
Old Shaft
Old Coal Level
RHYMNEY RAILWAY
WALNUT TREE BRANCH
Mort Chap.
CEMETERY
CARDIFF RAILWAY
Towing Path
Weir
Lock
Ford
Allotment Gardens
Taff's-well
Recreation Ground
Meth. Church
Chapel
Station
Chap.
Square Bog
Miners Hall
Viaduct
RHYMNEY BRANCH
Ill
900
200
300
400
500
100

The view from the Barry Railway viaduct, which towers above the valley, looking north across Walnut Tree Junction, with the River Taff on the left. The road along which the two men are walking became known as the Cardiff Road, and can be seen crossing over the Taff Vale Railway lines before going through the village of Taffs Well. This photograph, c1900, gives a clear view of the TVR station, as well as the Rhymney Railway's booking office, but that company's engine shed to its right and the sidings containing laden coal wagons and a brake-van are not so easily seen. On the extreme right are the internal lines leading into the forge works alongside. The Rhymney engine shed opened in 1858, and was closed by the GWR in September 1922. *Lens of Sutton collection*

that the neighbours can easily see what each other is doing.

In speeding along from Caerphilly Station, we observe Van Castle to the south-east. This ancient place, which is now in ruins, was the residence of Sir Edward Lewis, whose daughter Elizabeth married the Earl of Plymouth, through which marriage the land in this part of Wales came into the possession of that distinguished family which is now represented by the Honourable R. Windsor Clive, the present owner of those ancient domains.

Immediately after passing the woollen manufactory and mill, the ruins of Energlyn are seen on the left, and in another minute Pwllypant House, the residence of W. E. Williams Esquire, appears in sight, surrounded by rich meadows which reach to the river Rhymney, which divides the counties of Glamorgan and Monmouth. Skirting Coedybrain we pass Ty'n-y-graig and Darren-y-morthwyl, and soon reach Ystrad mill, whence we have a beautiful view of the noble mansion belonging to the Reverend George Thomas, the verdant fields, the majestic woods rich in foliage, and the great viaduct of Maes-y-cwmwr, over which the Taff Vale Extension, or loop line, passes to Pontypool, Hereford, and the north.

The viaduct appears beautifully grand, being more than a hundred feet high from the river, the houses underneath appearing like Lilliputian cottages, but the most remarkable feature in this bridge is the curve, designed undoubtedly to display the skill of the engineer and architect. Before reaching this viaduct Ystrad church is seen on the right, a recently built edifice in the parish of Llanvabon.

At the west end of the viaduct are situated the Hengoed Stations on the Rhymney and Hereford lines, that on the Hereford line

Left **An Ordnance Survey map of 1921 showing Walnut Tree Junction (lower right) beneath the Barry Railway viaduct, and the various railways winding their way up the Taff Valley.** *Crown copyright*

being reached from the Rhymney line by a short flight of steps.

To the east of this spot at the distance of about three miles, the traveller observes the whitewashed tower of Mynyddyslwyn Church. Starting up from here another recently built edifice is reached. This is a church, or chapel of ease, in the parish of Gelligaer, the ancient church being to the west of this place at a distance of nearly two miles. This was built for the convenience of the inhabitants of Pontaberpengam and the neighbourhood, where some thousands of underground workmen and their families reside.

Here are extensive collieries from which vast quantities of coal have been sent during these last thirty years to Newport by a tramroad which was made at the expense of a company of which Crawshay Bailey, Esquire, is the principal. A great number of collieries have been worked during the last century in the adjoining parish of Bedwellty, at Gellihaf and Gellideg, the upper seams of which are now worked out, so that these last-named places are at present deserted, and it will require a large amount of capital to sink to the lower veins before any reaction can take place in those localities.

The collieries between this place and Rhymney are of a modern date. As we approach Bargoed Station the grey and weather-beaten tower of Bedwellty Church is to be observed on top of the hill to the east of Bargoed Bridge.

Here is the little village of Pontaberbargoed surrounded by steep hills on either side, the sombre appearance of which casts a melancholy gloom over the mind of the beholder.

The Rhymney Valley now gets narrower and narrower, and after the last-named station is passed, it cannot be considered but a mere dingle, edged in by barren mountains, the outward aspect of which affords but a faint idea of their inward value.

The nearer we get to Rhymney the face of nature becomes more and more barren, she seems to deny her aid to vegetation, not a tree or a shrub seems to grow spontaneously, the mountain tops and sides being covered with a kind of peat which produces bilberries and heath in abundance. Here and there may be seen some trees which have been planted of late years, and extensive fields well cultivated, the verdure of which presents a striking contrast with the ruddy coloured surface of the adjoining commons and mountains.

Those fields, which are abundantly manured by the Rhymney Iron Company, afford large crops of hay for the use of their horses. When we observe those well-cultivated fields amidst such a vast extent of barren land, at such a high situation on the mountains, it convinces us at once that the whole of that land could be brought to bear rich crops of hay, oats, and barley, were the population to follow agriculture instead of excavating the bowels of the earth.

But to resume our journey, we have passed Tirphil Station, and immediately we arrive at the end of our excursion trip, in the midst of cinder tips, surrounded by forges and furnaces, clouds of smoke, and an abundance of dust.

Here thousands of people get their daily bread by digging and hammering, squeezing and rolling, sawing and shearing, hauling and driving; in fact, they seem as busy as a lot of ants whose hillock has just been disturbed by some wicked urchins.

Having visited the greatest part of the iron works we took a ramble through the place, which is not kept in the highest order of cleanliness, pigs being allowed about the streets, if streets they can be termed. Everybody here seems to build according to his own whim and caprice, without observing any regular order in the formation of streets, and the scavenger's cart is wholly unknown here, the roads being strewed with ashes and refuse from the houses in every direction.

Having seen all that we wished in this busy place, we returned by the evening train, and as we came in sight of the picturesque landscape in the Vale of Glamorgan it appeared to our mind more beautiful than ever, the contrast between it and the uncultivated and desolate hills which we had just left appeared to a much greater advantage, and filling the mind with ineffable delight.

Above Another view of Walnut Tree Junction, or Walnut Tree Bridge as it was originally known, from the viaduct, this time on the other side of the river on 11 July 1959. Skirting the hillside in the background is the former Barry Railway line to Penrhos Junction. The Taff Vale line can be seen running off to the left, as well as the line leading to Nantgarw Colliery, while the Rhymney line curves to the right to cross the canal and the Cardiff Railway line. A '56xx' Class engine with a mineral train is coming off the Rhymney line from Penrhos Junction to join the former TVR line, en route southwards. The Rhymney Railway engine shed now has the words 'Coal cutters' on its end wall, and the sidings and booking office can also be seen. The large group of buildings next to the sidings was known as the Garth Foundry in the 1920s, and some time later became South Wales Forgemasters. *B. J. Miller collection*

Below Looking south towards Cardiff, dominating the scene is the former Walnut Tree Viaduct, built and used by the Barry Railway; today only the piers are left In the centre is the Cardiff Road bridge, and on the right can be seen the Taff Vale Railway signal box, the second on this site. On the left can be seen the original Rhymney Railway booking office, with a short platform alongside; this building was in use as a permanent way office by British Railways when photographed on 13 July 1958. *H. C. Casserley*

Top Looking across the former Taff Vale lines past the signal box in January 1985, the Rhymney buildings are seen from an unusual angle. The former booking office, long used as a permanent way cabin, and the 7¼ milepost can be seen, behind which an oil drum sits on its wooden cradle. Behind the drum is the engine shed, once used to house the Rhymney banking engine, and providing the backdrop is the office block and buildings of South Wales Forgemasters, whose internal lines, set into concrete, as most industrial lines were, and barely visible, pass through the gate beside the engine shed. *Author.*

Middle This photograph of Walnut Tree Junction, looking northwards, shows on the right the end of the Rhymney Railway line after its long descent of the 'big hill' to join the TVR lines at this point. In the background a solitary British Railways 12-ton former pipe wagon is on the siding that runs behind the old booking office, at either end of which are two yellow-painted markers, the milepost and, at this end in the grass, an oval junction number, 12. Protecting the junction are lower-quadrant signals, one in the 'off' position for the former TVR down main line, while the other controls the down main to the down relief. The sidings and booking office were all demolished by British Rail at the end of 1987, and in February 1988 a 'park and ride' facility was installed on the site. During June of that year the lines on the 'big hill' were removed, and the ballast levelled; this was the beginning of a new era, as the branch became a cycle track and footpath, which today is part of the Taff Trail from Taff's Well to Caerphilly and beyond, with a tarmac surface and lined with fencing, trees and bushes. *Author*

Bottom On 11 June 1949 a former Rhymney Railway 'R' Class engine stands at Taff's Well. Formerly No 44, built by Beyer Peacock in 1921, works number 6100, it is seen here wearing its GWR number 40 and working as a banking engine for trains going up the 'big hill'. *F. T. Hornby*

In 1912 *The Railway Magazine* (Volume 31) published this article about the exploits of Mr Robert Weatherburn, a locomotive engineer who was employed by the Rhymney Railway during its early years, and who, 'while trying out an engine' in 1869, witnessed a 'wild run' down the 'big hill'. The following is an extract from the article, published under the title 'Leaves from the Log of a Locomotive Engineer':

> I well remember, amongst many others, a most remarkable occurrence when trying a new engine, one designed by Kitson & Company, for the Rhymney Railway. The order had been given at the time when the company was in low financial condition, partly if not wholly caused by the heavy tariff and restrictions imposed by the Taff Vale Railway over whose rails the Rhymney Company had at that time to travel in and out of Cardiff as far as Walnut Tree Junction, before they could touch their own territory.
>
> Before clearing the Taff Vale, both I and Mr John Kendal, the locomotive engineer, noticed a thud-like sound at every revolution of the wheels. We therefore arranged to stop at the first convenient place, on clearing the Taff, in order to examine and find out the cause. After leaving Walnut Tree Junction some distance, we availed ourselves of the loop or bypass provided for contingencies, and made a close examination. This resulted in my discovering six distinct flat places on the tyres of the wheels, and these I found afterwards were caused by the man in charge from Leeds (Shaw) putting on the powerful double-acting handbrake in order to assist the brakesmen when descending the Lickey Incline, on the Midland Railway, thus skidding the wheels. Being satisfied as to the cause, we were just about starting for the main line again (single track) when Mr Kendal, whose hearing was exceedingly keen, pointed with an alarming gesture up the distant hills, where to our surprise and dismay we saw, amidst dust and steam, a train coming on the track at an alarming speed.
>
> In another moment it was fully in view like an avalanche on wheels, with engine reversed and wheels braked, the fire

A distant view of a '56xx' Class engine bringing a train of loaded coal wagons down the Walnut Tree branch on the 'big hill' towards the junction at Taffs Well, en route southwards to the docks at Cardiff or Barry on 21 January 1965. The scar of the embankment above the train is the former Barry Railway line, which after crossing over the Taff Vale Railway lines by the Walnut Tree Viaduct skirted this hill for a short distance before it crossed over the Rhymney lines, via the viaduct at Penrhos (see page 32). *D. G. Thomas*

streaming in sparks from the numerous skidding wheels of the huge train, the wagons oscillating from side to side, scattering coal by the way. With unchecked speed and a gathering impetus, it sped like a hurricane in full blast on its way. The driver had recognised his chief, Mr Kendal, and as he flew by he pointed to the lever reversed, and put up both hands to show that all that was possible had been done.

'A wild run! A wild run!' cried our own men and for the first and only time I realised what I had often heard of in Wales. 'Pray God he does not foul the Taff, or we shall never hear the last of it,' said Mr Kendal.

The loading was, I heard afterwards, near a hundred and forty wagons, of coal and iron, and they lost control after leaving New Tredegar, running on to the Taff Vale, in spite of all efforts to the contrary.

Had the ready witted and keen-eared Mr Kendal failed to hear it for another half a minute, we should have been hurled to destruction and filled the track with coal, iron, and engines.

But 'All's well that ends well', such events were not infrequent, and as no lives were lost or damage done, the event, like many others, has passed into the limbo of forgetfulness, only to be dragged out to show the difference between the present and past order of railway working.

Mr Weatherburn goes on to say, 'When I first visited the Rhymney Railway, on the occasion just referred to, and presented my letter of

Left A former GWR '72xx' Class 2-8-2T engine hauls empties back up the valley past Penrhos Junction signal box in the summer of 1960. In the background, beyond the signal box, can be seen the connecting line between the Rhymney and Barry lines; the latter formerly crossed the Rhymney by the viaduct whose piers can be seen beside the train. Some of these '72xx' Class engines were rebuilds of the '42xx' Class, during the 1934-35 period, and the last had been withdrawn from service by 1965. This scene not only captures a forgotten moment of history, but also gives an insight to strangers visiting this area of just how beautiful this part of the Taff Trail is today. *A. Powell*

Left Penrhos Junction signal box on 9 October 1965, seen in its rebuilt GWR style. This box opened in 1935, and was closed by BR on 28 November 1968. *J. J. Davis*

introduction to Mr Cornelius Lundie, then General Manager, he sent for the engineer Mr Kendal, whom I found belonged to a well-known North of England family, and was highly respected. It is no exaggeration to say that no better or more enthusiastic mechanic ever lived than Mr Kendal.'

A few weeks after the 'wild run' incident, an engine trial was undertaken on a rebuilt engine from the Machen Works of the Brecon & Merthyr Railway. Mr Kendal was invited by Mr Simpson, the locomotive engineer of that company, to attend the trial as an honoured guest of the B&M. On the day of the trial, 10 June 1869, at Maesycwmmer, an accident occurred that resulted in the death of Mr Kendal and Mr Simpson, together with the others who were aboard the engine.

The first Caerphilly station had been situated at the rear of the Station Inn (see map below). This public house can still be seen, and even visited, located opposite the later-built Aber Halt. The part of Nantgarw Road that adjoined the station was renamed Station Road, but this station closed to passenger services on 1 April 1871, the same day that Cefn On Tunnel and the present Caerphilly station opened.

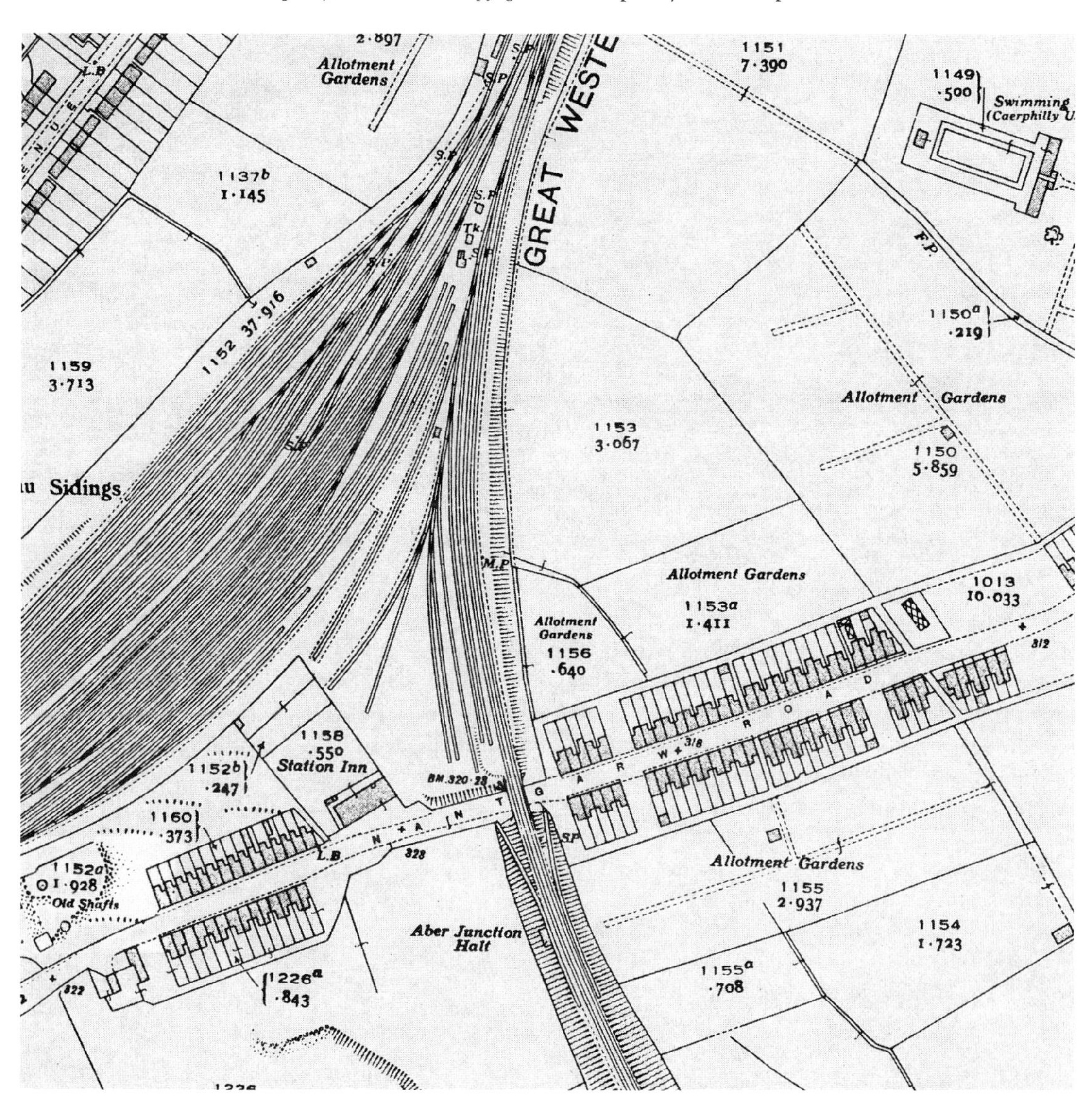

A 1937 Ordnance Survey map showing Beddau Sidings, the Station Inn (site of the original Caerphilly station) and Aber Junction Halt on Nantgarw Road on what became the main line to Cardiff via the new Caerphilly station. *Crown copyright*

Beddau Sidings, looking towards Aber Junction, on 26 April 1960. On the extreme right of this photograph in the distance is the Station Inn on Nantgarw Road and the site of the original Caerphilly station. *B. J. Miller collection*

Aber Junction signal box in September 1984. While the nameplate on this side gives the name in full, that on the other side reads simply 'AJ'. The box closed in May 1987. *Author*

The *Cardiff Times* of 15 May 1858 described the original station in an article headed 'Trip up the Rhymney Valley': 'Visitors to Caerphilly Castle would alight at this station and admire the bucolic scenery on the walk past neatly trimmed hedges and green fields after crossing Nantgarw Road.

Another article in the *Cardiff Times*, this time on 7 July 1860, gave this rather humorous account of people travelling to Cardiff from Caerphilly station, which at that time had been open just two years. A passenger told the reporter that '...whilst travelling from Rhymney to Cardiff, he was startled on arrival at Caerphilly Station to see the principal residents of the ancient town all eagerly rushing into the carriages. He naturally concluded that the French had made an attack on the town and captured the castle, thus all the important inhabitants of Caerphilly were making all convenient haste for Cardiff.'

Even at that date, some 45 years after Waterloo and the end of the war with Napoleon, the French were still clearly regarded as a threat!

The above extracts are from Mr G. G. Jones's excellent work, *Cronicl Caerffili*, No 5.

3. CAERPHILLY BRANCH

Right Ex-GWR 0-6-0 pannier tank No 9425, with an up-valley freight, takes the Caerphilly branch at Caerphilly West Junction on 26 April 1960; the line to the right leads to Aber Junction. The photograph gives a clear view of the signal box and signalman. The box closed in 1967. *B. J. Miller collection*

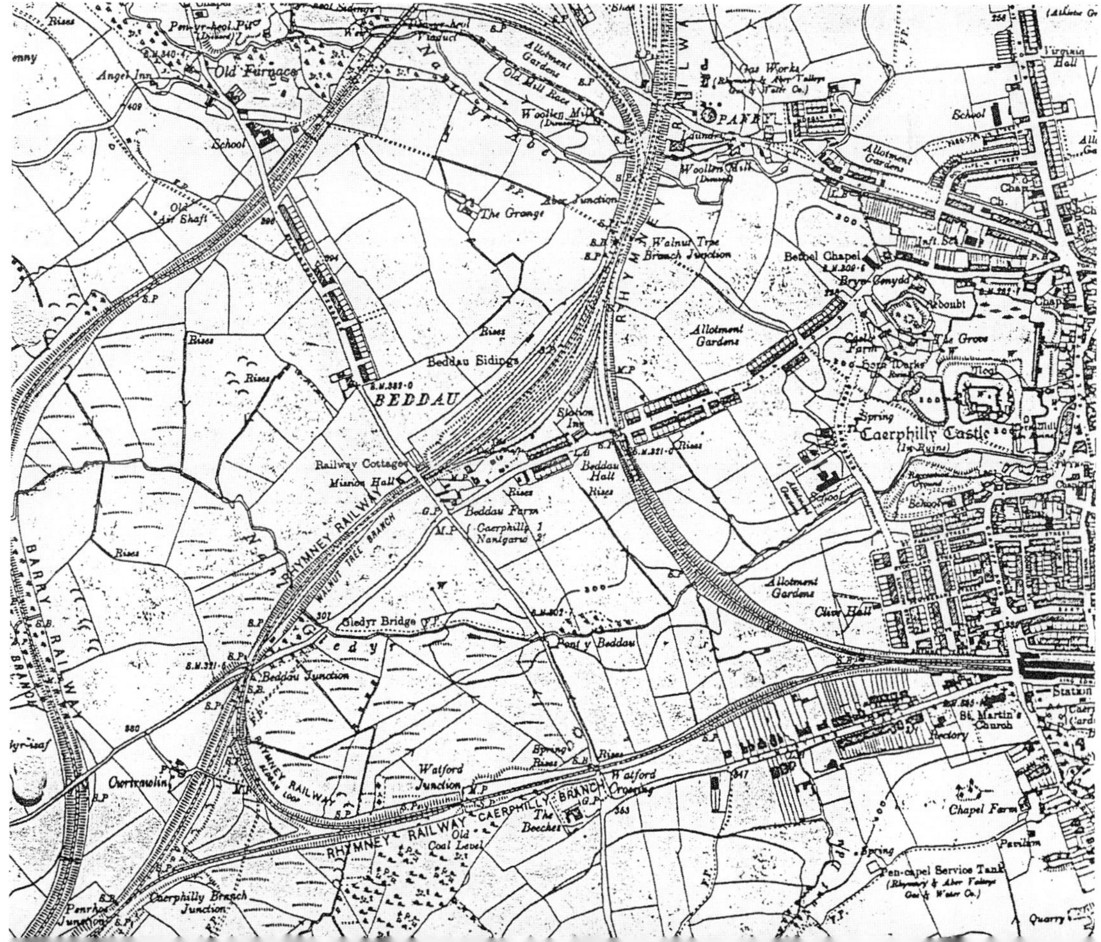

Below The Caerphilly branch ran between Beddau Loop Junction, on the original main line between Penrhos Junction and Walnut Tree Branch Junction (left), and Caerphilly West Junction (right) via Watford Crossing (centre). *Crown copyright*

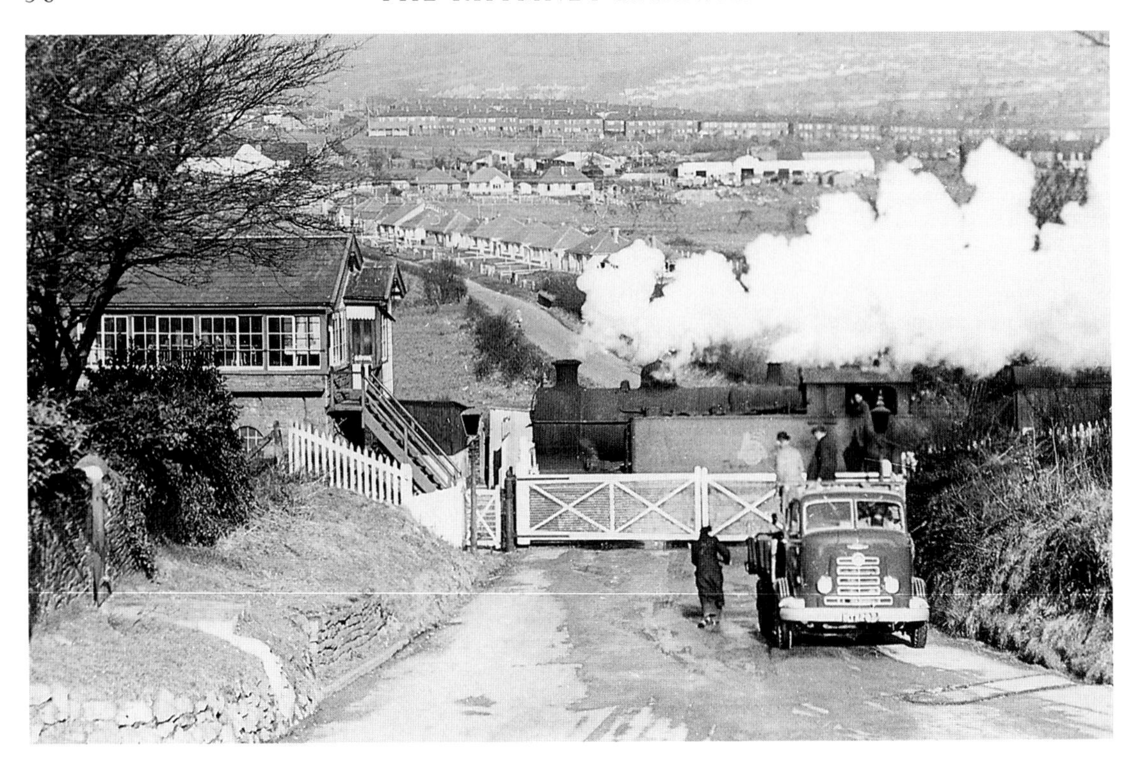

Above Between Caerphilly West Junction and Penrhos Junction was Watford Crossing and Watford Junction, where the line to Beddau Loop Junction diverged to complete the triangle of lines at this point. Former Rhymney Railway No 46 is seen here passing the level crossing working a Cardiff to Bargoed Pits freight on 16 February 1957. This 'R' Class engine, now carrying its GWR number 42, was built in 1921 by Beyer Peacock, works number 6102. Watford Crossing signal box closed on 1 May 1967. The lorry is a Commer, possibly a 3-tonner, a product of the Rootes Group. *B. J. Miller collection*

Below Watford Crossing, from an Ordnance Survey map of 1937. *Crown copyright*

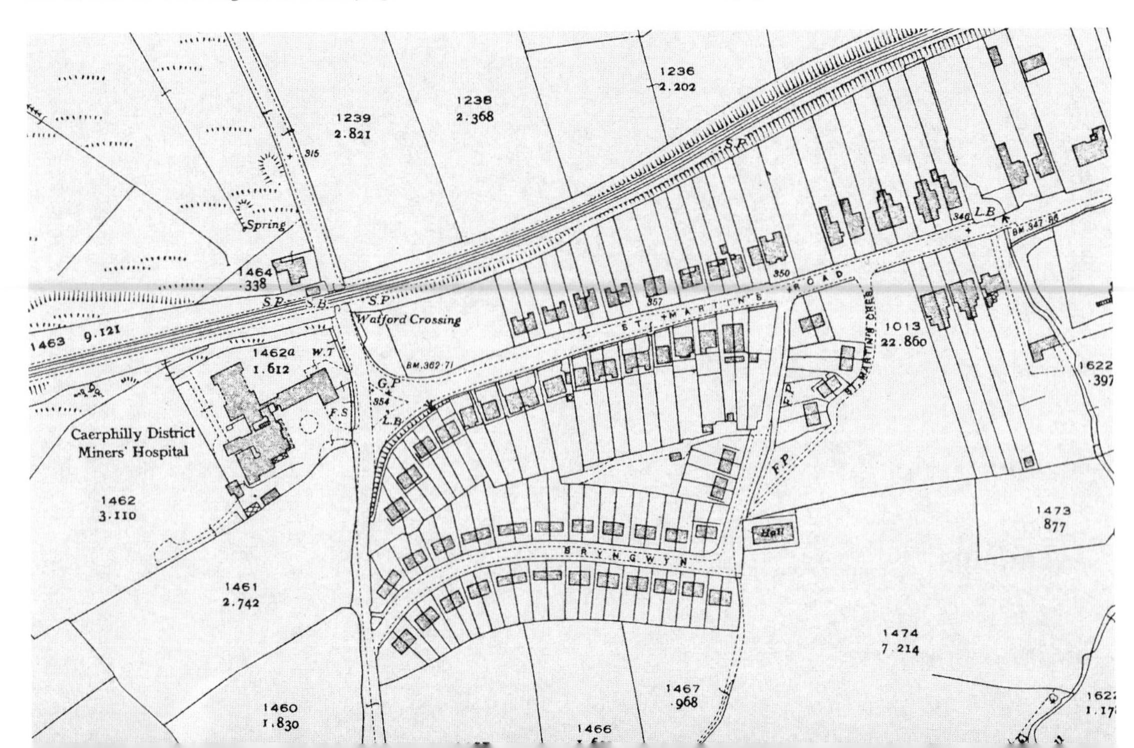

Top This is what being a railway photographer is all about! You chose a good viewing place, check the light, put the lens in focus, wind on the film, have a cuppa from your flask, then eat a sandwich or two, listening to the birds and feeling at peace with nature, waiting and hoping that something perhaps a little unusual will come along. And here we have it, another former Rhymney Railway 'R' Class 0-6-2T, GWR No 38, working a Cardiff Docks to Bargoed Pits service near Beddau Loop Junction. Its train comprises one sheeted wagon and a 16-ton former GWR ('Toad') brake-van. As Rhymney Railway No 42 the engine was built in 1921 at the works of Hudswell Clarke, works number 1439. Withdrawn by British Railways in 1957, it is seen here on its last but one journey before scrapping, on 4 October of that year. Rarely does one manage to get a photograph of a train driver, but here both driver and guard are seen, and if a friendly wave is given, the risk of getting cold or wet is worthwhile. *B. J. Miller collection*

Middle Also photographed at Beddau is former GWR '57xx' 0-6-0PT No 4679, on 26 August 1964. It was built in 1944 at Swindon Works, and withdrawn from service in 1965. *B. J. Ashworth*

Bottom An unusual track-level view of Beddau Loop Junction signal box, looking south towards Penrhos Junction, on 4 May 1964. The nameplate is an original Rhymney Railway enamel example, with white letters on a blue background. *M. Hale*

4. DARRAN AND DERI BRANCH

Above The Darran and Deri branch opened in March 1864, originally as a single line, but doubled in 1909. It closed to passenger services on 31 December 1962. This photograph, taken from Bargoed station on 28 October 1952, shows in the background the North Junction signal box, and a Brecon passenger train just passing it en route up the branch. North Junction signal box closed on 9 November 1970. *M. Lloyd*

Below Ogilvie Colliery Sidings were located a short distance from Bargoed North Junction, and in the background of this view, c1900, is Bargoed Viaduct. Ogilvie Colliery closed in March 1975. Nearby Groesfaen Colliery opened in about 1906, and closed in 1968; Groesfaen South and North signal boxes closed, like Bargoed North, in November 1970. The sidings are a hive of activity, accommodating a mixture of Rhymney Railway vans and open wagons, some carrying planks of wood, of which two are being unloaded. In the foreground are a few private owner colliery wagons, one of which is being swept out, perhaps to receive the wood. Two of the colliery wagons are from the Llanbradach Colliery, while one looks to be from the Lewis Merthyr Colliery; its livery would be black with white lettering, with a red and white emblem on the side door. *Author's collection*

Above Photographed at Ogilvie Colliery Sidings, at the side of engine No 5697, before returning with a full load to Radyr Junction, driver Mr Viv Crabb and his fireman, Ray Cook, take time to pose for this photograph in about 1963. *V. Crabb*

Below Opened on 16 May 1935 as Ogilvie Village Halt, this photograph shows the re-named Ogilvie Halt on 2 May 1959, with a Newport to Brecon train at the platform. These 'pagoda'-type shelters were found all over the GWR system, being cheaply made from corrugated tin sheeting. Originally designed for the storage of bicycles, they quickly became popular as waiting rooms, booking offices and storage sheds, and many a small station or halt had them. Ogilvie Halt closed to passenger and goods services on 31 December 1962. *B. J. Miller collection*

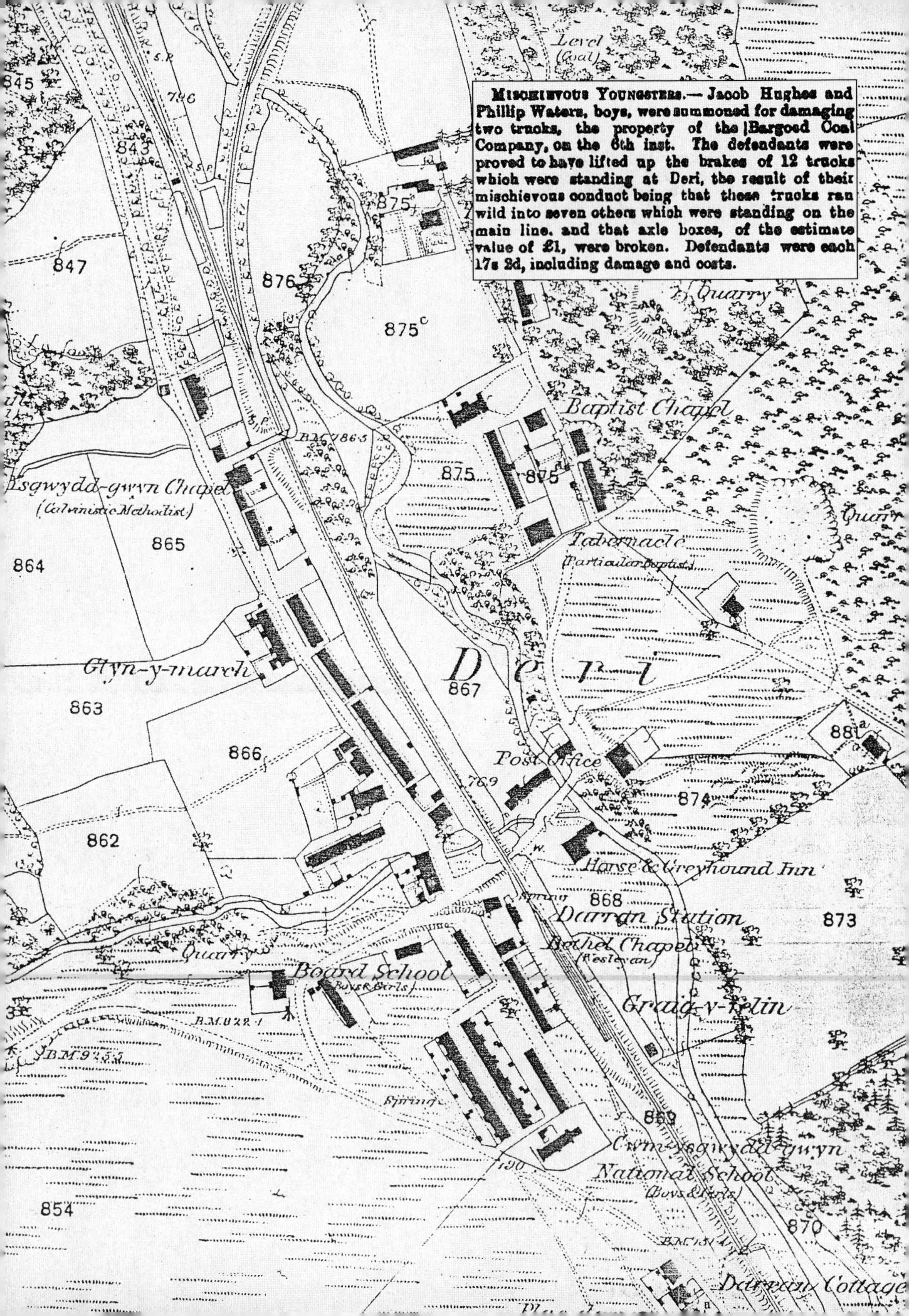
Level (Coal)
Quarry
Baptist Chapel
Esgwydd-gwyn Chapel
(Calvinistic Methodist)
Tabernacle
(Particular Baptist)
Quarry
Glyn-y-march
Deri
Post Office
W.
Horse & Greyhound Inn
Spring
Darran Station
Bethel Chapel
(Wesleyan)
Craig-y-felin
Board School
(Boys & Girls)
Quarry
Spring
Cwm-Esgwydd-gwyn
National School
(Boys & Girls)
Darran Cottage
845
843
796
847
876
875
875c
875
875
865
864
863
866
862
867
769
874
881a
868
873
869
870
854
190
B.M. 786·5
B.M. 829·1
B.M. 925·3

Mischievous Youngsters.— Jacob Hughes and Phillip Waters, boys, were summoned for damaging two trucks, the property of the Bargoed Coal Company, on the 6th inst. The defendants were proved to have lifted up the brakes of 12 trucks which were standing at Deri, the result of their mischievous conduct being that these trucks ran wild into seven others which were standing on the main line. and that axle boxes, of the estimate value of £1, were broken. Defendants were each 17s 2d, including damage and costs.

Left **An 1873 Ordnance Survey map showing Darran, later Darran & Deri station.** *Crown copyright*

Inset **'Mischievous conduct' at Deri: from the** ***Pontypridd Chronicle*****, 16 August 1884.** *Pontypridd Library*

Darran & Deri station, looking north, with a permanent way gang working on the up line in about 1950. The station closed to passenger services on 31 December 1962, and eventually to goods traffic on 23 August 1965. In the distance can be seen a farm crossing bridge, now preserved. *Locomotive & General Railway Photograph Co*

The station as seen from a train on 24 December 1962, providing a rather good view of the down-line waiting room. The gas lamps on the platform are of a different style from those seen in the previous photograph, which were of the lantern type. Today the station site and trackbed are part of the Cwm Darran Park and cycle track, from Deri to Bargoed. *F. T. Hornby collection*

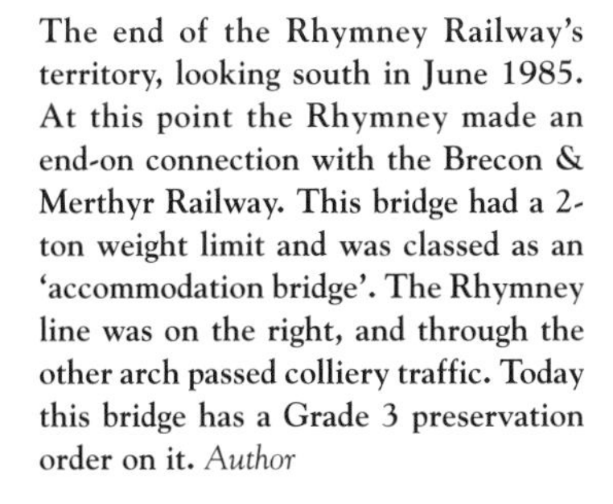

The end of the Rhymney Railway's territory, looking south in June 1985. At this point the Rhymney made an end-on connection with the Brecon & Merthyr Railway. This bridge had a 2-ton weight limit and was classed as an 'accommodation bridge'. The Rhymney line was on the right, and through the other arch passed colliery traffic. Today this bridge has a Grade 3 preservation order on it. *Author*

5. PENALLTAU BRANCH

A series of meetings were held by the Rhymney Railway's Board of Directors during 1870 and 1871 to discuss plans for this branch. On 24 May 1870 tenders were considered, with a time limit for completion of 1 February 1871. A tender from Mr T. J. Waller was accepted, at £3,798. On 30 May 1871 the branch was ready for inspection by the Board of Trade, but on 11 July it was announced that the opening had been postponed for a month. Finally, on 5 September 1871 a report from the Board of Trade authorised the Penalltau branch to be opened for passenger traffic.

Above Two views of Ystrad Mynach South Junction signal box on 20 September 1987. A complex structure designed to get the rods and wires down to track level from the box's elevated, set-back position can be seen. The box controlled the junction of a short line that joined the Rhymney line with the Taff Vale Extension Railway at Penalltau Junction. *Author*

Left In this photograph taken from the car park of Ystrad Mynach station on the same day, the main line is just out of sight on the left, while on the right can be seen Class 37 No 37799 hauling a rake of fully loaded 'merry-go-round' hoppers en route from the Deep Navigation Colliery to Aberthaw Power Station. The train is standing on the Penalltau branch, waiting to join the main line at South Junction a short distance further down. Behind the hopper wagons is the site of Ystrad Mynach station's Dowlais platform (see also the map on page 86). *Author*

Above This photograph, taken on 6 June 1953 from a passing train, shows the down-side Dowlais platform at Ystrad Mynach, with a GWR corrugated tin shelter as the waiting room; swan-neck lighting and the GWR monogrammed platform seats complete the scene. Today nothing is left except bushes and brambles. *The late N. L. Browne, courtesy of Mr F. T. Hornby*

Below This is the up platform looking towards Penalltau Junction on 26 May 1958, of stone construction, unlike the down-side platform. *M. Hale*

Above Former GWR '56xx' Class 0-6-2T No 5673 descends the Penalltau branch between the Tredomen Works and Ystrad Mynach, crossing the A472 road on its way down from Penalltau Junction on 26 August 1964. The size of these British Railways-built 24½-ton open wagons restricted their use, so they were only used on routes between selected collieries and power stations, a lesson learned by Sir Felix Pole and the GWR with its 20-ton coal wagons. No 5673 was built at Swindon Works in 1926, and withdrawn in 1965. *B. J. Ashworth*

Below On 27 April 1957, between Tredomen Works and Penalltau Junction signal boxes, '56xx' Class No 5636 climbs towards Penalltau with empties for Ocean Colliery. The line above the engine is the Pontypool Road to Aberdare line of the Taff Vale Extension Railway, which the Rhymney Railway line will join at Penalltau Junction. Tredomen Junction signal box was opened by the GWR in 1922, and closed on 11 July 1966; Penalltau Junction signal box closed on 15 June 1964. No 5636 was a Swindon product of 1925, and was withdrawn in 1962. *B. J. Miller collection*

The Rhymney Railway had running powers over the Taff Vale Extension line from Penalltau Junction to Quakers Yard, which enabled its trains to reach its Abercanaid and Taff Bargoed branches. Although neither Nelson & Llancaiach nor Quakers Yard were Rhymney Railway stations, both being on the Taff Vale Extension, they are included as they played a part in the history of the Rhymney company.

Above Nelson & Llancaiach station is seen here from the east on 31 July 1965. The signal box opened on 1 July 1912, and closed on 8 September 1968, the station having closed to passenger services on 15 June 1964. The line from Ystrad Mynach to Nelson & Llancaiach was singled on 15 September 1968. *F. T. Hornby collection*

Below Quakers Yard High Level station was the last Taff Vale Extension station that the Rhymney Railway passed through en route to and from Merthyr. Once beyond here it entered joint Great Western and Rhymney Railway territory again, on the Abercanaid branch. This station was known generally as High Level from 1891 to 1897, but it was many years before the title became official. Seen here with its staff, c1905, the station closed entirely (to all services) on 15 June 1964. *Lens of Sutton collection*

6. RHYMNEY BRIDGE BRANCH

Top The branch from Rhymney northwards to Rhymney Bridge Junction on the LNWR's Merthyr-Abergavenny line, and thence to Nantybwch, was jointly owned by the Rhymney Railway and the LNWR. The section between Rhymney and Rhymney Bridge station closed to passenger services on 21 September 1953, and to goods traffic on 23 September 1963. This is Rhymney Bridge on 6 June 1953. Today the station lies buried beneath tons of rubble, and is covered by a roundabout to form part of the A465 trunk road. *The late N. L. Browne, courtesy of Mr F. T. Hornby*

Middle Caught on film on 5 January 1958 is a special SLS train of railway enthusiasts at Rhymney Bridge station on the last day of services along the former LNWR Merthyr-Tredegar-Abergavenny line. The station had already closed to goods services on 22 November 1954, and from 6 January 1958 would be closed completely. *S. C. L. Phillips, courtesy of D. K. Jones collection*

Bottom Rhymney Railway 'K' Class No 82 leaves Rhymney Bridge station with a passenger train on 25 July 1922. This engine was built in 1897 by Sharp Stewart & Co, works number 4262, was re-numbered by the GWR as 117, and was withdrawn some time between 1925 and 1934. *R. S. Carpenter*

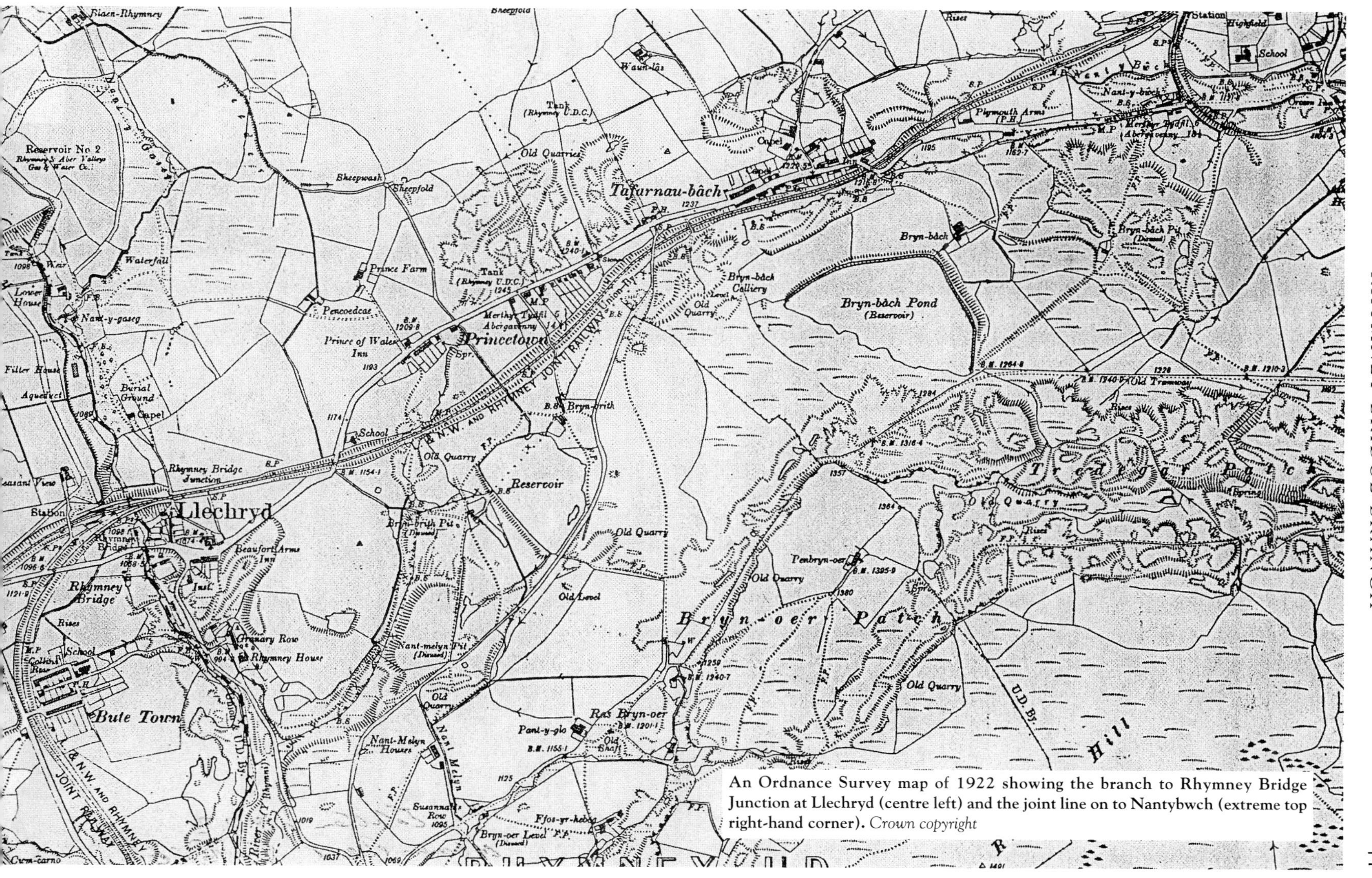

An Ordnance Survey map of 1922 showing the branch to Rhymney Bridge Junction at Llechryd (centre left) and the joint line on to Nantybwch (extreme top right-hand corner). *Crown copyright*

Top At Nantybwch the LNWR's line south towards Newport left the Abergavenny-Merthyr line. On 30 November 1957 a Newport train stands at the branch platform. This was as far as the Rhymney Bridge joint line went, and the station had run-round facilities that enabled Rhymney trains to be reversed without trespassing on LNWR lines. *S. C. L. Phillips, courtesy of D. K. Jones collection*

Middle Earlier in 1957, on 14 August, Nantybwch No 1 signal box, of LNWR design, was photographed. This was a good day for the photographer – usually in this area, being at the head of the Sirhowy valley, it is raining or covered by mist! *B. J. Miller collection*

Bottom The Newport platforms at Nantybwch, with No 40171 having banked a miners' train into the station on 14 August 1957. Today there is nothing left to indicate that a station was ever here – all is grassed over, with only a children's playing area to mark the location. *B. J. Miller collection*

7. TAFF BARGOED BRANCH

This was another Rhymney Railway and Great Western Railway Joint line, and ran from Nelson & Llancaiach station on the Taff Vale Extension line up Cwm Bargoed to Dowlais. It opened for goods and mineral traffic on 10 January 1876, and to passenger services on 1 February.

Above Ffaldcaiach signal box was just north of Nelson & Llancaiach. On 26 August 1964 former GWR '56xx' Class 0-6-2T No 5691 stands beside English Electric Type 3 (later Class 37) No D6820, fitted with air brakes. This signal box closed on 30 January 1965, the same year that the '56xx' was withdrawn, having been built at Swindon Works in 1927. *B. J. Ashworth*

Right A little further north was Trelewis Platform seen here on 28 June 1963. It opened 10 July 1911, and closed to all services on 15 June 1964. This view shows the up-side waiting room. *J. J. Davis*

Waterfall
Quarry
Old Quarry
Quarries
Old Incline
Trial Shaft
Bont Newydd
Pumping Station
Coal Level
Pontnewydd
Filter Beds
U.D. Ry
Ocean Deep Colliery
St. Mary's Church
Air Shaft
Trelewis
G.W.R. AND RHYMNEY JOINT LINE
TAFF BARGOED BRANCH
Tirbach
Viaduct
Glyn Bargoed
Pont Square
Melin-cajach
Corn Mill
Treharris
Gas Works
Bargoed Taf
Capel Horeb
Chapel
Quarry
Pandy Cottages
Quarries
Efail Singrug
GREAT WESTERN RAILWAY
Park House
Brooklands
Singrug
TRAMWAY

Left An 1897 Ordnance Survey map with 1914 additions, showing the GWR and RR&GWR Joint lines running parallel from Taff Bargoed Junction (in the extreme bottom right-hand corner), before parting company near Trelewis. *Crown copyright*

Inset This is the down-side accommodation at Taff Merthyr Colliery Halt, looking south on 28 June 1963. As with Trelewis Platform, it is difficult to find any trace of the halt today. In August 1965 a landslip occurred that weakened the banking on the up side, leading to the decision to single the line. *J. J. Davis*

Top This is Bedlinog station at about the turn of the 20th century looking south towards Trelewis village, with a mixture of Rhymney Railway vans and a sheeted wagon in the goods siding behind the station picket fence. The height of the signal box allowed a clear view of the line and was also governed by the steep gradient of the road and road bridge alongside. *Lens of Sutton collection*

Middle Bedlinog station and goods shed are seen here after closure, on 16 May 1965; although the station itself still looks unchanged, the goods shed has started to lose its planking. *H. Leadbetter*

Bottom Another view of Bedlinog's goods shed on the same day, this time viewed from the yard side. For the railway modeller a model of this station or goods shed would enhance any layout. *H. Leadbetter*

An Ordnance Survey map of the Bedlinog area in 1897. *Crown copyright*

Top A passenger train from Nelson calls at Bedlinog on 26 September 1960. The station closed to goods traffic on 7 October 1963, and for passenger services on 15 June 1964. In its heyday, with traffic from the pits and travellers on business, the nearby Station Hotel must have done a roaring trade. Today only the station footbridge and a piece of the platform remain, and the goods yard area is used as a coach terminus. The ex-GWR '56xx' Class engine, No 5603, was built at Swindon Works in 1924, and withdrawn in 1964. *R. M. Casserley*

Middle '56xx' Class No 5677, built at Swindon in 1926 and withdrawn in 1965, leaves Bedlinog with a Dowlais Cae Harris passenger train, c1964, the fireman and signalman preparing to exchange the single-line tokens. The aqueduct carrying water over the line, seen here in front of Bedlinog signal box, is still in situ today. *L. Bryant*

Bottom An engineers' train behind another '56xx' Class, No 5688, was the last train to run from Bedlinog to Dowlais Cae Harris in about 1965. Photographed at Bedlinog, this engine was withdrawn in the same year, having been built in 1927. *Mrs E. Williams*

Top A wintry scene at Bedlinog Colliery Junction signal box, in about 1960. Bedlinog Pit Workmen's Platform, located nearby, was opened some time after 1915, and had closed by 1938. *Mrs E. Williams*

Middle The shafts for Bedlinog Colliery were sunk during the period 1881-83, with production starting in the latter year. It is seen here c1895, and closed in 1956. The coal wagons in the foreground have the word 'DOWLAIS' on their sides. *The late John A. Owen collection*

Bottom Another view of Bedlinog Colliery, c1910. Known as the Big Pit, the No 1 shaft was 600 yards long and 15 yards deep, and the No 2 shaft was only 80 yards less in length. Nantyllyn Colliery, located between Bedlinog Colliery and Cwmbargoed, opened in September 1928 and closed in 1954. *Mrs E. Williams*

Top A somewhat indistinct 1922 photograph of Rhymney Railway 'S1' Class No 33 with a coal train passing Cwmbargoed signal box. Built in 1920 by Hudswell Clarke, works number 1409, this engine was initially numbered by the GWR as 605, then later re-numbered 91, and was withdrawn in 1954. *LCGB, Ken Nunn Collection*

Middle A clearer view of Cwmbargoed Station Signal Box, c1969. *Author's collection*

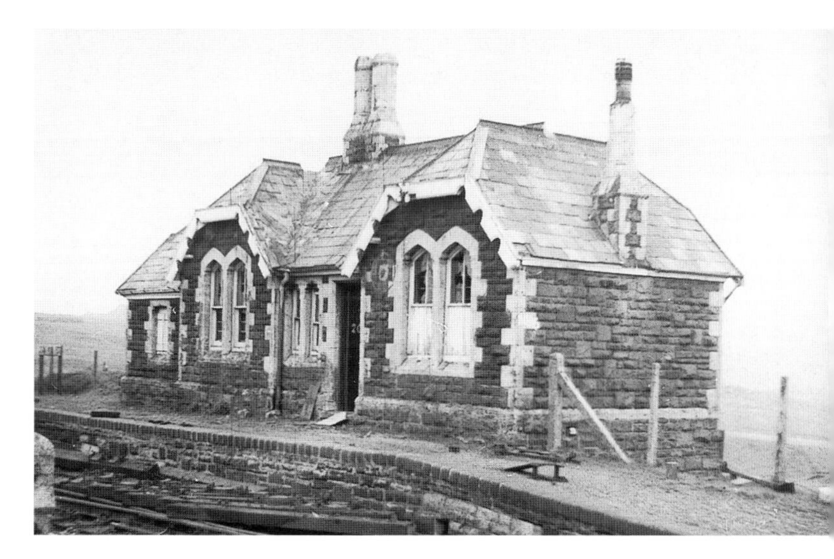

Bottom Cwmbargoed station is seen here on 15 May 1965, after closure. The station had an unusual, almost 'Dutch'-style roof that made it very distinctive; however, considering the inclement weather in the area, it was probably a sensible design. Bedlinog station had a similar type of roof. Cwmbargoed closed to goods traffic on 7 October 1963, and to passengers on 15 June 1964. *M. Lloyd*

Overleaf A 1938 Ordnance Survey map of the Merthyr Tydfil area. The Taff Bargoed branch comes in from Cwmbargoed (centre right) and curves round into Dowlais Cae Harris station top right, just to the right of the Dowlais Iron Works. *Crown copyright*

CYFARTHFA PARK
Cyfarthfa Castle
Swimming Bath
Weir
Spring
800
Gwaun-farren
Lodge
Gwaelod-y-garth Cottage
Gwaelod-y-garth House
PEN-Y-DARREN
Pavilion
Band Stand
Lodges
Park Cottage
Tramroad Lane
School
Nant Morlais
Old Tramway
Bradley Row
TYDFIL'S WELL
Park Row
Castle Square
The Avenue
Electric Power Station
(Merthyr Electric Traction & Lighting Co.)
Tramway Depot
Brick Works
PEN-YARD
Shaft
Coal Level
INCLINE
Pen-y-darren House
PEN-Y-DARREN PARK
Football Ground
Infant School
Neath 22 M.P.
Stone Circles
Schools
Taff Brewery
MERTHYR TYD
GWENITH
Schools
Cyfarthfa Cinder Tip
GEORGE TOWN
Christ Church
Infirmary
CEMETERY (Disused)
PONTMORLAIS
Spring
Cae-Mari-dion
Garw Pits (Disused)
Reservoir
School
Workho
Band Stand
Pant-y-ffy
THOMAS TOWN
Sew Mill
Old Ironstone Level
Old Shaft
Ynys-fach Iron Works (Disused)
Lock
Station
Brick Works
CEMETERY (Disused)
Old Pound
Llwyn-celyn Junction
Llwyn-celyn
Old Engine House
Ironstone Drift
Old Coke Ovens
CAE-DRAW
Old Gas Works
PEN-YR-
DOWLAIS RAILWAY
TWYN-YR-ODYN
Coal Drift
Air Shaft
Upper Wern
Lower Wern
Old Coal Level
RHYD-Y-CAR
Weir
Coal Level
Coal Drift
Nant Rhyd-y-car
Engine House
Rhyd-y-car Pit (Disused)
Old Rhyd-y-car
Ysgubor-newydd
Old Limekiln
Isolation Hospital
(Merthyr Tydfil Corporation)
Stone
Air Shaft
Pen-cae
Reservoir
Reservoir
Merthyr Junction
Lower Colliers Row
Old Coal Drift
Old Ironstone Level
Old Coal Level
Coal Drift
Tank
The Willows
Gas Works
(Merthyr Tydfil Gas Co.)
Brandy Bridge Junction
Incline
Prospect House
Glyn-mil Drift
Old Shaft
Pen-yard House
Pen-yard Row
Air Shaft
Glyn-mil Pit No.1 (Disused)
Spring
Coal Level
GWR MERTHYR BRANCH
Weir

Dowlais Iron Works
Dowlais Great Tip
Brick Works
Reservoir
Old Shaft
Engine Shed
Longtown
Old Ironstone Level
Dowlais Junction
No. 7 Pit
Old Quarry
Old Level
Ton-y-ffald
Old Air Shafts
G.W.R. ZIG ZAG BRANCH
No. 4 Pit
Old Reservoir
TAFF BARGOED BRANCH
G.W.R.
MINERAL RAILWAY
No. 2 Pit
Spring
Rises
Mansfield Terrace
No. 1 Pit
Air Shaft
Aqueduct
MOUNTAIN HARE
No. 6 Pit
Old Air Shaft
Old Pit
Ffos-y-frân
Reservoir (Merthyr Tydfil Corporation)
Slaughter House
Old Quarry
Isolation Hospital (Merthyr Tydfil Corporation)
Pen-coedcae
Old Coal Level
New Pit
Old Quarries
Old Ironstone Level
Clyn-mil Pond
Old Kiln
Old Gravel Pit
Sheepfold
Upper Clyn-mil
Aqueduct
Waun Level
Cairn
Clyn-mil Pit No. 2

Above Class 37 No 37162 and a permanent way gang are on ballasting duties at the site of the former Cwmbargoed station, c1983. This diesel-electric locomotive was built in 1963 at the Robert Stephenson & Hawthorn Works, Darlington. *M. Davies*

Below On 14 May 1988 the Monmouthshire Railway Society's 'Spring Railtour' passes Ryan's opencast mining site at Cwmbargoed in rather isolated countryside, at the top of the world, or so it seems. The train is composed of two three-car DMU sets coupled together and full of enthusiasts; the leading set in No T303. Ffochrhiew Pits, located on a short spur east of Cwmbargoed, opened in July 1897, and were renamed Fochriw Pits some time after November 1915, then Fochriw Colliery in September 1928. West of Cwmbargoed was Penydarran Platform, opened in September 1928 and closed in 1954. *B. Morris*

Above Only occasionally does such a photographic moment happen, and this one has it all: the engine with an old clerestory coach attached, and passengers leaving the station except for one, who is patiently waiting by the lamp-post for his son. The date is 6 June 1953, the location is Dowlais Cae Harris Station, the engine is No 5655, and the train is bound for Nelson & Llancaiach. This '56xx' Class engine was built in 1926 and withdrawn in 1965. *The late N. L. Browne, courtesy of Mr F. T. Hornby*

Below Another view of Dowlais Cae Harris station about seven years later. It closed to the handling of goods and mineral traffic on 7 October 1963, and for passenger services on 15 June 1964. *Lens of Sutton collection*

Above We are now looking south from Dowlais Cae Harris station in about 1960, towards the engine shed, which is out of sight to the right of the picture. One of the British Railways posters reads 'Please help to keep this station TIDY', which is a bit ironic – the station is to be kept tidy while the slag tips behind make the town untidy! Today nothing is left of this once busy station, the site just an area of neglected ground. *Lens of Sutton collection*

Below A 6 June 1953 view of Dowlais Cae Harris engine shed, with a '56xx' Class engine alongside the water crane. The shed opened in 1876 and closed in December 1964. *The late N. L. Browne, courtesy of Mr F. T. Hornby*

Dowlais Iron Works

Dowlais Iron Works first became associated with railways when it supplied the iron rails for the Stockton & Darlington Railway in 1821, and although it had opened more than half a century earlier, the supplying of iron rails and other products to the railway companies was a real beginning. By 1856 the Bessemer process was being introduced, and the Dowlais Iron Works started to manufacture steel. Eventually the works merged with the Patent Nut & Bolt Company of Birmingham, owned by Arthur Keen, and later became Guest, Keen & Company.

In 1902 a further merger took place with Nettlefold Limited, and the new company was known as Guest, Keen & Nettlefold (GKN). Later still the works became the Dowlais Foundry of the British Steel Corporation, but closed in November 1987.

Today there is little left; to the people of Dowlais, who have known hard times, the closing of the works was a loss that was irreplaceable.

Top **A snatched photograph of wagons crossing Dowlais High Street from the works to Dowlais Cae Harris sidings on 19 March 1973.** *The late Norman Parry*

Middle **The Ivor Works internal line led to the Dowlais Iron Works along the back of the houses in the town. Seen here is *Sudbrook*, a Dowlais Works engine, at the rear of houses along Merthyr Road in 1933.** *Mid Glamorgan Libraries*

Bottom **An undated photograph of Dowlais Iron Works' engine *Peacock* No 2.** *Mid Glamorgan Libraries*

Above A heavy load moves along Gwernllwyn Road, Dowlais Works, in about 1963. *The late John A. Owen collection*

Left A general view taken from the entrance of Dowlais Works, c1971. The internal lines can be seen quite clearly in the foreground, embedded in the road. *B. Morris*

Extracts from the *Pontypridd Chronicle* of 5 July 1884 (*below*), concerning the effects on Dowlais Works of a severe lack of rainfall in July, and a 'terrible accident' reported on 16 August 1884 (*left*). *Pontypridd Library*

DOWLAIS.

ACCIDENT.—A few minutes after eight o'clock on Monday morning, a terrible accident occurred in the Lower Works, Dowlais, to two men, named John Devine and Dan Kennedy, both aged about 50. Near the engine-house at the top of the incline a large number of old iron castings and scraps are gathered, that they may be broken up by a kind of circular hammer known as the "ball." The ball is of tremendous size, and is worked by steam power, while the iron thus broken up is taken away by the wagons belonging to the Dowlais Iron Company. It was at this ball that the two unfortunate men worked at the time specified. All had gone well for some time until Devine and Kennedy went up to one of the trucks for some purpose just at that moment that another truck was coming up. The inevitable result was that they were crushed between the trucks, both being fearfully injured.

The rainfall on Saturday proved quite a God-send, not only to the thirsty garden plants, but also to the workmen of the district who have suffered severely from slackness of work consequent upon the scarcity of water. Dowlais Works were on the point of suspending operations owing to the absence of motive power and a portion of the works had already stopped. They have now, however, resumed work, and we hope it will be a long time before they suffer similarly again.

RECKLESS REVENGE BY A BOY AT DOWLAIS.

PLACING A BRICK ON THE RAILWAY.

At Merthyr petty sessions, on Saturday, David John Llewelyn, a lad of only fourteen years, was summoned for wilfully placing a brick on the railway at Dowlais to the danger of the persons travelling thereon.—Mr Arthur James prosecuted, and Mr J. Plews defended.—David Jenkins, an engine-driver in the employ of the Dowlais Company, said he was a driver between Vochrhiw and Pantywaun, and on the 27th of December the defendant, who was employed on the same line to oil the points, got on the engine at Pantywaun. Whilst the fireman was attaching a chain to pull some trucks the lad turned on the steam and the chain snapped. For this he was kicked off the engine by the fireman, and he afterwards walked down the line. As the engine was proceeding it ran into a siding leading into a quarry, the fireman being unable to turn the points as a brick had been placed thereon. When first charged the lad denied having placed the brick there, but afterwards admitted doing so, giving as a reason that the fireman kicked him.—Mr Plews argued that there had been no endangering of life as the engine only ran into a siding—The Stipendiary committed the lad for trial at the next quarter Sessions.

Left 'Reckless revenge' at Dowlais: an item from the *Pontypridd Chronicle* of 19 January 1884. *Pontypridd Library*

Above Dowlais Works during reconstruction work in about 1865-70. A steam crane is at work on the right, and a mixture of wagons are removing the rubble from the demolished buildings. *The late John A. Owen collection*

Below In about 1905 new blast furnaces are being built at Dowlais Iron Works. Nearest the camera is one of the works' end-tipping slag wagons, while on the right is a rake of side-tipping wagons being shunted by one of the works engines; one of the wagons can be seen dumping its load. Some of these slag wagons would have been horse-drawn – the ironworks had an intensive establishment of stables nearby. *The late John A. Owen collection*

Above A postcard of about 1900-08 shows Dowlais Iron Works with its extensive internal sidings. *The late John A. Owen collection*

Below A steam crane in use at the Sleeper Plant of Dowlais Works, c1924. *The late John A. Owen collection*

Above On 27 June 1912 King George V and Queen Mary visited Dowlais Iron Works. Seen here with the Royal Train at Dowlais furnaces, awaiting Their Majesties, are works engines *Arthur Keen* and *Sandyford*, their nameplates changed for the occasion to *King George V* and *Queen Mary*. The driver of one of the engines is believed to have been Mr Twm Cardi. *The late John A. Owen collection*

Right The red carpet and dignitaries await the visit by the King and Queen. In the background, due to their sheer size and height, the blast furnaces seem to loom over everything and everyone. *The late John A. Owen collection*

Right Their Majesties alight from a Taff Vale Railway Directors' carriage at the start of their visit. *The late John A. Owen collection*

8. ABERCANAID BRANCH

This branch was another Rhymney Railway and Great Western Railway Joint line, and ran from the GWR at Quakers Yard High Level through Aberfan to the GWR's Merthyr-Hirwain (later Hirwaun) line at Joint Line Junction, just east of Merthyr Tunnel.

QUAKER'S YARD.

THE NEW RAILWAY.—On Monday afternoon one the engines belonging to the Rhymney Railway Company ran over the line of railway which the Rhymney Railway Company and the Great Wes- tern Railway Company are making from here to Merthyr. One line nas been laid and completed so far as to enable the engine to run right through into the Cyfarthfa Works. Mr R. Evans, assistant traffic manager on the Rhymney Railway, with Mr Inspector Llewelyn and other officials of the above company, accompanied the engine, which took a guard's van through. It is very probable that the above line will be opened to-morrow (Thursday).

Above 'The New Railway': from the *Pontypridd Chronicle*, 3 January 1885. *Pontypridd Library*

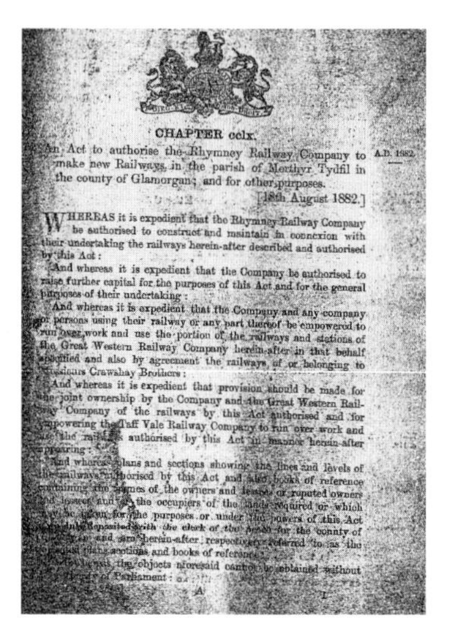

CHAPTER ccl x.

An Act to authorise the Rhymney Railway Company to make new Railways in the parish of Merthyr Tydfil in the county of Glamorgan; and for other purposes. A.D. 1882.

[18th August 1882.]

WHEREAS it is expedient that the Rhymney Railway Company be authorised to construct and maintain in connexion with their undertaking the railways herein-after described and authorised by this Act:

And whereas it is expedient that the Company be authorised to raise further capital for the purposes of this Act and for the general purposes of their undertaking:

And whereas it is expedient that the Company and any company or persons using their railway or any part thereof be empowered to run over work and use the portion of the railways and stations of the Great Western Railway Company herein-after in that behalf specified and also by agreement the railways of or belonging to Messieurs Crawshay Brothers:

And whereas it is expedient that provision should be made for the joint ownership by the Company and the Great Western Railway Company of the railways by this Act authorised and for empowering the Taff Vale Railway Company to run over work and use the railways authorised by this Act in manner herein-after appearing:

And whereas plans and sections showing the lines and levels of the railways authorised by this Act and also books of reference containing the names of the owners and lessees or reputed owners and lessees and of the occupiers of the lands required or which may be taken for the purposes or under the powers of this Act [illegible] with the clerk of the peace for the county of [illegible] and are herein-after respectively referred to as the [illegible] plans sections and books of reference:

[illegible] the objects aforesaid cannot be obtained without [illegible] of Parliament:

Above **The Act of Parliament dated 18 August 1882 authorising the Abercanaid branch.** *Author's collection*

Below A former GWR '66xx' Class 0-6-2T heads a coal train on the joint line near Quakers Yard in about 1954. *P. J. Garland, R. S. Carpenter collection*

Right **An Ordnance Survey map of 1948 showing the joint line heading north through Aberfan. Seen bottom right is the short spur from Merthyr Vale Junction, re-crossing the River Taff to reach Merthyr Vale Colliery, just across the river from Aberfan station.** *Crown copyright*

Aber-fan
Merthyr Vale
River Taff
Merthyr Vale Colliery
Station
Goods Shed
Zion Chapel
R.C. Church
Gas Wks.
Schools
Pant-glas
Old Limekiln
Dan-y-deri
Old Colliery
Old Quarry
Air Shaft
Old Coal Levels
Cemetery
Mort. Chapel
Capel Smyrna
Quarry
Trial Shaft
Perthi-gleision
Hafod Tanglwys Uchaf
Hafod Tanglwys Isaf
Old Coal Shaft
Old Air Shaft
Old Coal Level
Spring
Rises
700 Yds.
600 Yds.
500 Yds.
Rifle Range
Target
Old Target
Nant Aber-fan
Aber-fan-fach
Aber-fan-fawr
Locks
Canonbie
Station Hotel
Capel Calfaria
Ynys-Owen
Oaklands
Black Lion Gates
Mount Pleasant
Allotment Gardens
School
New Cottages
Trial Level
Mynydd y
Sheepfold
Old Shaft
Tarren y gigfran
Twyn Brynbychan
Cistfarn
Maerdy
Cefn y

Three early views of Aberfan station, looking north. The first, c1900, shows the road bridge across the line; the girder supporting the stonework of this bridge was inscribed 'Brymbo, 1884'.

Perhaps a decade later, station staff pose for their photograph, complete with the stiff starched collars that were much in evidence in those days. The station nameboard is different; it looks as though the station name has been added above the original board, which simply read 'For Merthyr Vale'. In later years the board was revised again, as seen in the third view, dated c1924.

The station closed to passenger services on 12 February 1951, and to goods traffic on 1 November 1954. It was similar to Llanishen in that it had a booking office at road level, and those wishing to travel up the valley had to cross by the road bridge after purchasing a ticket. *Lens of Sutton collection (2)/B. Morris*

The next stop north of Aberfan was Troedyrhiw, re-named Troedyrhiw Halt by the Great Western Railway on 1 July 1924; it closed to passenger services on 12 December 1951, and to all traffic on 1 November 1954. Pontygwaith Halt closed entirely on 12 November 1951.

Castle Pit, between Troedyrhiw Halt and Gethin Pit Platform, opened in July 1897, and closed some time after 1915; Gethin Pit Platform itself opened some time after 1915, and had closed by September 1928. Both Castle Pit and Gethin Pit were owned by the Cyfarthfa Iron Works.

Above Rhymney Railway 'K' Class saddle tank No 86, built by Sharp Stewart in 1897, works number 4266, heads a Merthyr to Cardiff passenger train near Abercanaid in about 1922. The engine was later re-numbered 127 by the GWR, and withdrawn some time between 1925 and 1934. *LCGB, Ken Nunn Collection*

Below Another saddle tank, this time Rhymney Railway 'J' Class No 76, is seen with another Merthyr to Cardiff service near Abercanaid at about the same time. Also a Sharp Stewart product and built in 1894 as works number 4040, it later became GWR No 109, and was withdrawn at about the same time as No 86 above. *LCGB, Ken Nunn Collection*

ABER-CANAID
Old Coal Shaft
Football Ground
Graig Pit (Disused)
Station
Graig Cottage
Reservoir
Old Coal Level
Old Air Shaft
Graig
Waunwyllt Colliery
Tramway
Reservoir
Old Air Shaft
ABER CANAID
Reservoir
Engine House
Reservoir (Disused)
Glamorganshire Canal (Disused)
Old Coal Level
Old Coal Level
LOWER PENTRE-BACH
Infant School
Baptist Chapel
Football Ground
Plymouth Feeder
MINERAL RAILWAY
TAIBACH
DYFFRYN
Dyffryn Boiler Works
Old Ironstone Level
Old Level
Castle Level (Coal)
Iron Works (Site of)
Trial Shaft
Pen-rhiw-'rohen
MERTHYR
Springs
Rises
Reservoir
Castle Houses
Buarth-y-mynydd
Plantation Square
Rises
Rises
Rises
Rises
Cnwc
Old Quarries
Old Quarry
Springs
Pwll-gwelli
Stone
800
900
1000
700
600

Left A 1948 Ordnance Survey map showing the upper part of the joint line towards Abercanaid (top left). Note how close together are the joint line and the Glamorganshire Canal on the west bank of the Taff, and the Taff Vale line on the east side.

During 1985 construction work began on the new A470 trunk road from Abercynon to Merthyr, thus avoiding the old Merthyr road and the villages connected with that rather narrow and winding route. This was an extension of a road that originated in Cardiff, using most of the former Glamorganshire Canal route as far as Abercynon, and which would now be extended to run along the west bank of the River Taff using most of the trackbed of the former Abercanaid branch. *Crown copyright*

Above A Rhymney Railway passenger train leaves the station at Abercanaid, en route for Cardiff, in about 1922. This station opened on 1 April 1886, and was re-named Abercanaid & Pentrebach on 9 September 1913, reverting to just Abercanaid under the GWR on 1 July 1924. *LCGB, Ken Nunn Collection*

Below Another view of Abercanaid station, looking south at about the turn of the 20th century. An abundance of staff seem to have appeared for the photograph, and with a well-cultivated flower border they are obviously taking a great pride in the appearance of their station. The usual enamel advertising signs decorate the picket fencing. The station closed for passenger services on 12 February 1951, and to goods traffic on 9 May 1960. As at Aberfan, the girder supporting the bridge was inscribed 'Brymbo, 1884'. For many years a few half-hidden platform slabs remained to show the position of the station, but today there is nothing left of the area, having been covered by the extension of the A470 trunk road. *Lens of Sutton collection*

Abercanaid station is seen again at the centre bottom of this 1901 Ordnance Survey map, and just left of centre is Joint Line Junction (beside 'Glyn-dyrys Pond'), where the line from Quakers Yard joined the GWR's Merthyr-Hirwaun line. Merthyr Tunnel on the latter route commences in the bottom left-hand corner. *Crown copyright*

Above On the left is the signal box at Joint Line Junction, with a Brecon & Merthyr engine passing with a train on the line from Hirwaun, en route to Merthyr. The line nearest the camera is the Rhymney and Great Western Joint line of the Abercanaid branch. *Mid Glamorgan Libraries*

Below North of the junction, mineral lines ran to Merthyr's Cyfarthfa Iron Works. Rhymney Railway 'J' Class saddle tank No 9, built by Sharp Stewart in 1894, works number 4039, is pulling a workmen's train at the Cyfarthfa Works in the early 1920s. Re-numbered 86 by the GWR, it was withdrawn some time between 1925 and 1934. Cyfarthfa Colliery Platform, near Abercanaid, opened in July 1897, and closed some time after 1915. *LCGB, Ken Nunn Collection*

RAIL MAKING AT CYFARTHFA WORKS.

The first consignment of steel rails turned out from Cyfartha passed on Tuesday and Wednesday over the new line of railway from Merthyr to Quaker's Yard, and was conveyed by the Rhymney Railway Company's engines, *via* Penallta and Ystrad Junctions, over the Rhymney Railway to Cardiff for shipment. Twenty wagons were despatched.

Above Another Rhymney Railway saddle tank, No 82 of the 'K' Class (built by Sharp Stewart in 1897, works number 4262) is seen on another workmen's train at the Cyfarthfa Works. Becoming GWR No 117, it was also withdrawn between 1925 and 1934. *LCGB, Ken Nunn Collection*

Left Traffic from Cyfarthfa over the new joint line: from the *Pontypridd Chronicle* of 29 May 1885. *Pontypridd Library*

Below Works engine *Cyfarthfa* at the Iron Works, c1890. *Mid Glamorgan Libraries*

9. ABER BRANCH

The Aber branch to Senghenydd was opened for passenger services and mineral traffic on 1 February 1894, and coal from this valley was shipped all over the world from the docks at Cardiff, Penarth and Barry. In 1902 the total amount of coal and coke carried to Barry Docks was 1,075,000 tons, which by 1908 had increased to 1,250,000 tons. After 1908 the tonnage carried was very heavy indeed; in that year a total of 785,000 tons was carried to the docks at Penarth. Yet it nearly did not happen, for nearly 25 years earlier, at a Rhymney Railway board meeting on 12 July 1870, the minutes record a decision to abandon the Gledyr branch, and not to proceed any further with the Aber branch, beyond land already purchased. The land purchased in 1870 amounted to a short length of track leading from Aber Junction to the Tregibbon Colliery, a distance of just 42 chains.

The two pits at Senghenydd, York and Lancaster, were sunk in 1892 at a cost of £25,000; they came under the ownership of the Universal Collieries group, which in turn was taken over in 1900 by the Lewis Merthyr Consolidated Colliery Companies. Grief swept through the villages of Abertridwr and Senghenydd on 24 May 1901 when the Lancaster Colliery suffered an explosion that killed 81 men, but that was nothing compared to the second Lancaster Colliery disaster of October 1913. A deadly pocket of gas, invisible and undetected, trapped between the layers of coal, exploded to cause the worst disaster in the history of British coalmining, when a total of 439 men and boys lost their lives. After the initial explosion the pit burned inside itself – truly Dante's Inferno. Lancaster Colliery closed in 1930 with the industrial depression of the time, while York Colliery lasted until 1961.

The permanent way yard at Aber Junction, with its stock of rails, sleepers and fencing, was situated to the north of Caerphilly, close to Walnut Tree Branch Junction on the main line. The yard opened with the Aber branch on 1 February 1894, and was where the coal traffic for Cardiff, Penarth and Barry Docks was separated. Aber Junction is seen here 90 years later, looking north in September 1984; the main line up the Rhymney Valley is on the right, and the former Aber branch on the left. As can be seen, the breaking up of the junction has already started. *Author*

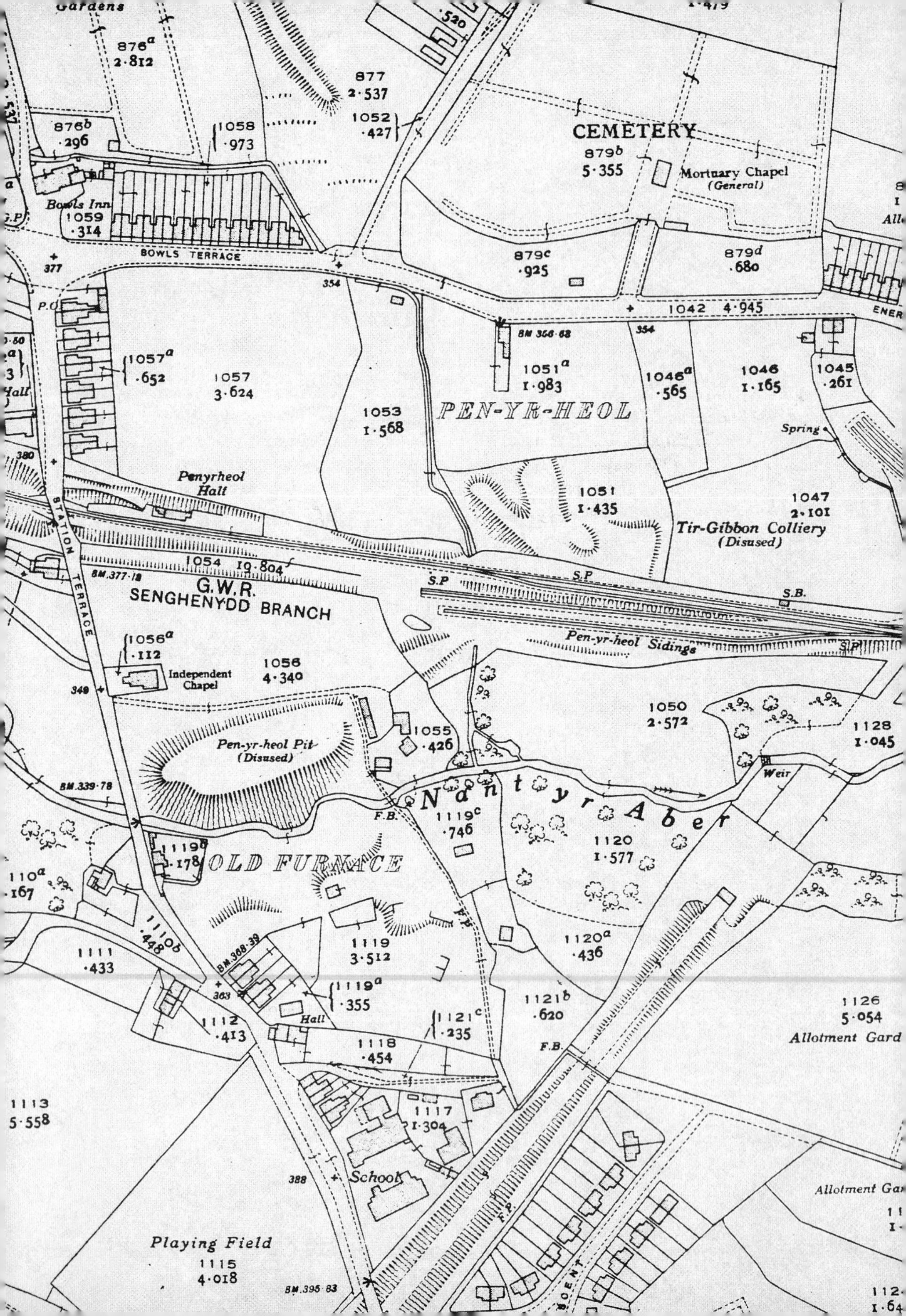

CEMETERY
Mortuary Chapel (General)
Bowls Inn
BOWLS TERRACE
PEN-YR-HEOL
Penyrheol Hall
STATION TERRACE
G.W.R. SENGHENYDD BRANCH
Tir-Gibbon Colliery (Disused)
Pen-yr-heol Sidings
Independent Chapel
Pen-yr-heol Pit (Disused)
Nant yr Aber
Weir
Spring
OLD FURNACE
Hall
School
Playing Field
Allotment Gard
Allotment Gar

Left Penyrheol Halt and sidings, from an Ordnance Survey map of 1937. *Crown copyright*

Right Penyrheol signal box and signalmen, c1900. *Lens of Sutton collection*

Below Penyrheol Halt, looking east towards Aber Junction, on 10 July 1958. The halt had closed to goods traffic on 16 July 1957, but passenger services lasted until 15 June 1964, although the line was used for the handling of Windsor Colliery traffic until that pit's closure in 1976. This colliery was sunk in 1895, production starting in that year. Following its closure coal from its seams was extracted via Nantgarw Colliery, which opened in 1915, and closed in 1986. By the late 1980s only a short piece of platform remained, and today there is nothing to be seen of the halt or the trackbed, both erased by nature. The late eminent photographer H. C. Casserley stands on the platform on the left. *R. M. Casserley*

Recreation Ground
Reservoir
(Rhymney & Aber Valleys Gas & Water Co.)
Senghenydd
Old Coal Level
Quarry
Goldre
Paro-newydd
Reservoir
Cefn-llwyd
Blaen-y-flarch
Congl. Chap.
St. Peter's Church
St. Cenydd's Church
Gelli-fanadlog
Tan-y-Bryn
Bapt. Chap.
R.C. Ch.
Windsor Hotel (P.H.)
Ty'n-y-parc
Cae'r-llwyn
Bryncoed
Windsor Colliery
Old Quarry
Garth
School
Quarries
CAER
Schools
Recreation Ground
Aber-tridwr
Mission Hall
Coed Ty'n-y-parc
Windsor Place
Hendrederwen
Nant Ilan
G.W.R. ABER BRANCH
Pont yr Aber
Cwm yr Aber
Pont y Felin
Windsor Terrace
Cwm-byr Reservoir
Cwm-byr Quarry
Filter Beds
Old Coal Level
Old Air Shafts
Old Coal Level
Old Quarry
Coed Cae
Graig

Left The Aber branch is seen swinging north through Abertridwr and past Windsor Colliery to Senghenydd in this Ordnance Survey map of 1947. *Crown copyright*

Top This is Abertridwr station looking north, c1910. The station opened on 1 February 1894 as Aber, and was renamed Abertridwr on 26 June 1899. On the down platform a porter is sorting out mail bags lying on the ground, while the waiting room can be seen on the up side. The station closed to passenger services on 15 June 1964, and to goods on 1 March the following year. *Lens of Sutton collection*

Middle An RCTS excursion calls at Abertridwr in about 1971, comprising two three-car DMU sets, the leading one being No B560. This may have been the last excursion to use the branch before the rails were lifted. Today this area is landscaped with nothing to show what once was. *B. Morris*

Bottom The goods shed at Abertridwr, c1971, looking rather abandoned. *B. Morris*

Overleaf Railway and urban development at Senghenydd between 1900 (*left*) and 1915. *Crown copyright*

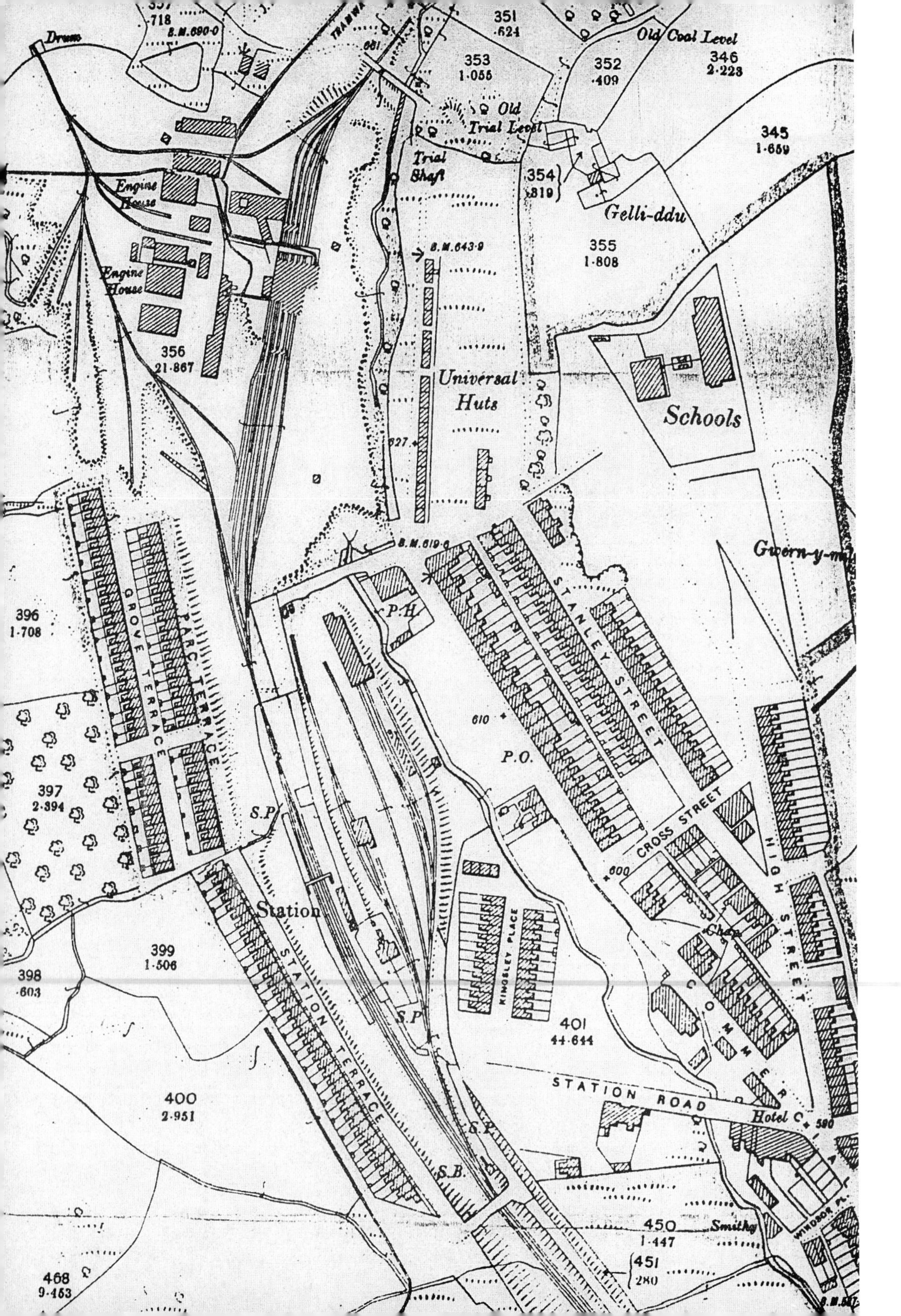
Drum
Engine House
Engine House
Old Coal Level
Old Trial Level
Trial Shaft
Gelli-ddu
Universal Huts
Schools
Gwern-y-mil
P.H.
P.O.
GROVE TERRACE
PARC TERRACE
STANLEY STREET
CROSS STREET
HIGH STREET
Station
STATION TERRACE
KINGSLEY PLACE
STATION ROAD
COMMERCIAL
Hotel
Smithy
WINDSOR PL.
S.P.
S.B.
Chap.

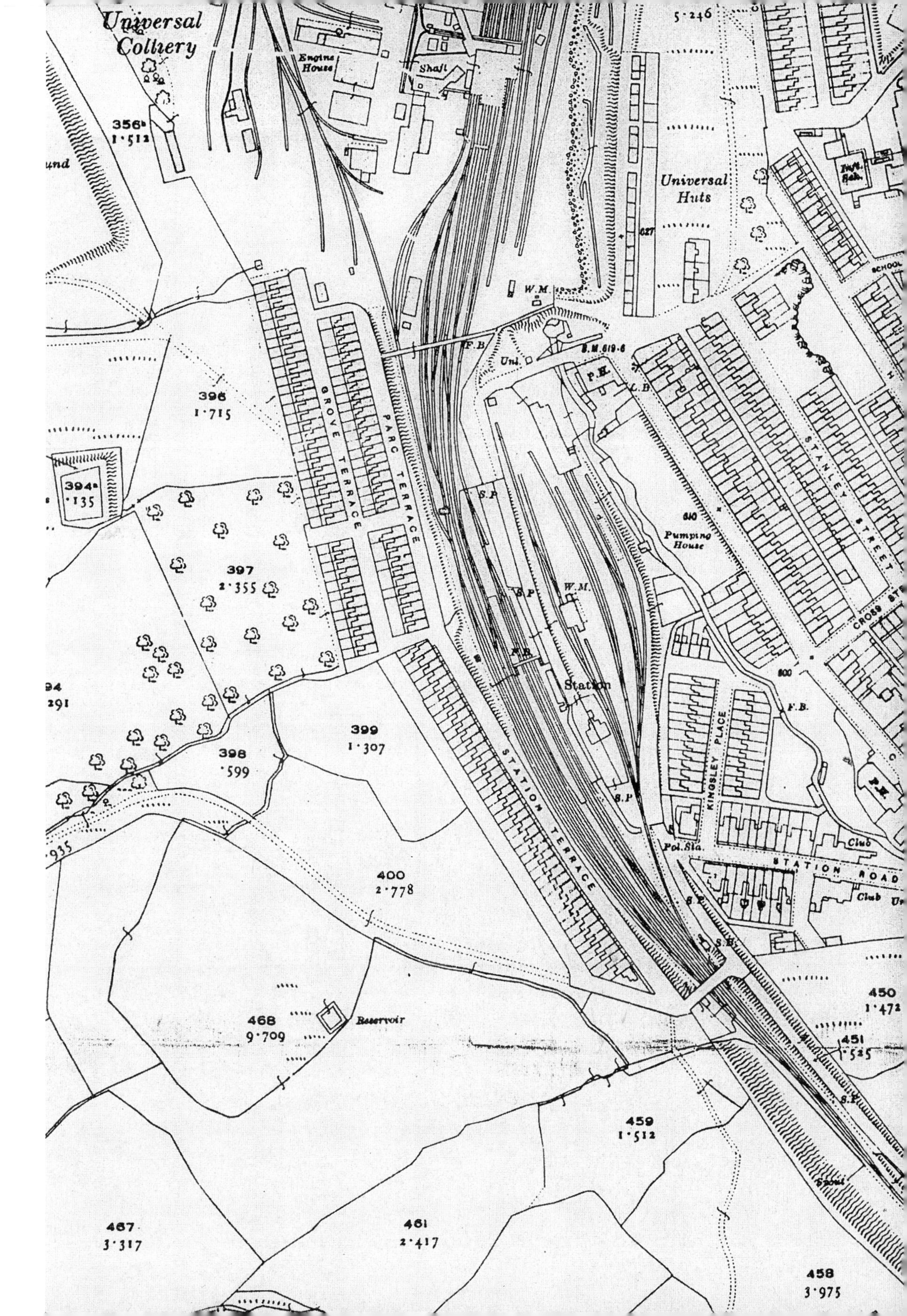

Universal Colliery
Engine House
Shaft
5·246
356b
1·512
Universal Huts
W.M.
F.B.
B.M. 619·6
Uni.
P.H.
L.B.
396
1·715
GROVE TERRACE
PARC TERRACE
STANLEY STREET
School
394a
·135
S.P.
610
Pumping House
397
2·355
S.P.
W.M.
F.B.
CROSS ST
Station
600
F.B.
394
·291
399
1·307
398
·599
KINGSLEY PLACE
STATION TERRACE
S.P.
P.H.
Pol. Sta.
Club
STATION ROAD
Club
·935
400
2·778
S.P.
S.B.
450
1·472
468
9·709
Reservoir
451
1·525
S.P.
459
1·512
Spout
467
3·317
461
2·417
458
3·975

Above Senghenydd goods shed on 28 June 1963, with Universal Collieries in the background. *J. J. Davis*

Below This early view of Senghenydd station is dated c1904. A passenger train is slowly approaching the station, while the solitary passenger waits for it to come to a stop. Behind him, on the down platform, a cart has been tipped into the upright position. The Rhymney Railway saddle tank is No 53 of the 'I' Class, built in 1884 by Sharp Stewart, works number 3182, re-numbered 625 by the GWR, and withdrawn between 1925 and 1927. Sunlight Soap and Kingov flour are being advertised, and the two gas lamps are of the lantern style. In the colliery sidings private owner wagons can be seen; one is a Lewis Merthyr Colliery wagon, built to carry a 15-ton load. The station was originally styled 'Senghenith', but the name was changed to Senghenydd on 1 July 1904, and it can be seen that the last three letters on the station nameboard have been amended fairly recently. *Author's collection*

Two photographs of an autotrain from Caerphilly at Senghenydd station on 21 May 1955. The first, looking north, shows the driving compartment in the end carriage. The second view shows the engine at the other end, 2-6-2T Prairie tank No 5568, built at Swindon Works in 1929 and withdrawn in 1963. The train stands at the down platform, almost ready to return, and to the right of the engine can be seen the up platform and Station Terrace. The station opened with the branch on 1 February 1894, and closed to goods traffic on 2 July 1962, and to passenger services on 15 June 1964. *F. T. Hornby*

Above A hillside vantage point gives a good general view of the Senghenydd station area, c1894, the lines and buildings contrasting well against the whiteness of the snow. The signal box can be seen on the extreme right, and the goods yard is at the rear of this station. What is not yet evident are the collieries and their sidings, although the area that will be used for them already looks prepared and level. Senghenydd signal box closed in 1963, and the engine shed, opened in 1894, was closed by the GWR on 23 May 1931. *Mid Glamorgan Libraries*

Below By 1915 the colliery sidings are quite extensive. At the front of Station Terrace are the private owner colliery wagons of the Lewis Merthyr Consolidated Collieries, while a Rhymney Railway saddle tank is shunting a mixed rake of vans and wagons in the goods yard. The engine shed can be seen in the centre, while over in Commercial Street the shops are doing a good business, judging by the amount of shoppers outside them. In the bottom right-hand corner is a whitewashed detached house, which is the police station. In the centre of the colliery's network of lines, between the station and colliery, is the footbridge that enabled pedestrians to cross over this busy network from Parc Terrace to the end of Commercial Street. Today the station, sidings and collieries have gone and the area landscaped – a housing estate now covers everything, and only the Station Terrace road bridge crossing the line remains. *Author's collection*

10. CYLLA AND YSTRAD BRANCHES

Also known as the Penrhiwfelin branch, the Cylla branch opened for coal traffic in 1906 following the sinking of Penalltau Colliery in 1905 and its opening the following year, and was extended a further 2 miles in 1909 when Penrhiwfelin Colliery opened. Mineral traffic on the branch was controlled by Ystrad Mynach North Junction signal box. However, a long time prior to this, on 13 November 1893, North Junction had opened for traffic via the Ystrad branch to Hengoed West Junction on the Taff Vale Extension of the GWR's Newport, Abergavenny & Hereford line. North Junction signal box closed on 20 September 1976, and Penalltau Colliery in 1991.

Right **Part of an announcement in the *Evening Express* newspaper of 27 November 1894 covering the Act to be heard in Parliament on 21 December 1894, dealing in part with the building of the Cylla branch.** *South Glamorgan Libraries*

Below **Estimate of expenses incurred in the making of the Cylla Branch prepared for the Act of 1885.** *South Glamorgan Libraries*

In Parliament.—Session 1895.

RHYMNEY RAILWAY

(CYLLA BRANCH).

ESTIMATE OF EXPENSE.

	Miles.	f.	chs.	Whether Single or Double.
Length of Line	2	6	3·14	Single.

Earthworks:	Cubic Yds.	Price per Yd. s. d.	£. s. d.	£. s. d.
Cuttings—Rock				
Soft Soil	272,000	1 1	14,733 6 8	
Roads	445	1 6	33 7 6	
TOTAL			14,766 14 2	14,766 14 2

		£. s. d.
Embankment, including Roads, 72,600 *Cubic Yards*		nil.
Bridges—Public Roads	*Number* 3	4,000 – –
Accommodation Bridges and Works		6,642 –
Viaducts		nil.
Tunnels		nil.
Culverts and Drains		1,100 – –
Metallings of roads and level crossings		100 – –
Gatekeepers' houses at level crossings		—
Permanent way, including fencing: Miles. f. chs. 2 6 3·14 at	Cost per Mile. £. s. d. 2,500 – –	6,273 2 6
Permanent way for sidings, and cost of junctions		4,000 – –
Stations		4,000 – –
	£.	41,581 16 8
Contingencies	10 per cent. (say)	4,158 3 4
		45,740
Land and buildings	A. R. P. 34 0 0	4,760 – –
	TOTAL £.	50,500

say £. 50,500.

COL. LUNDIE,
G. A. LUNDIE,
Engineers.

Evening Express

TUESDAY, NOVEMBER 27, 1894.

IN PARLIAMENT.—SESSION 1895.

RHYMNEY RAILWAY

(New Railway in the County of Glamorgan; Compulsory Purchase of Lands and additional Lands; Tolls, &c.; Revival and Extension of Time for the Purchase of Lands for, and Completion of, certain Railways authorised by the Rhymney Railway Act, 1890; Abandonment of Railways authorised by, and repeal of, the Rhymney Railway Act, 1888; Additional Capital; Creation and Issue of New Stock in substitution for Existing Ordinary Stock; Conversion of certain Preference Stock; Amendment or Repeal of Acts; and other purposes.)

NOTICE IS HEREBY GIVEN, that application will be made to Parliament in the ensuing session by the Rhymney Railway Company (hereinafter called the Company), for an Act for the following, or some of the following among other purposes, that is to say:—

1. To empower the Company to make and maintain, in the county of Glamorgan, the Railway and works hereinafter described, with all proper stations, sidings, junctions, bridges, approaches, works, and other conveniences connected therewith, that is to say—

A railway in the parishes of Llanfabon and Gelligaer, in the county of Glamorgan, commencing in the parish of Gelligaer by a junction with the main line of the Rhymney Railway, at a point on that railway 17 yards or thereabouts, measured in a northerly direction from the northern abutment of the bridge, situated near and northward of the Ystrad Mynach Station of the Company, and carrying the said railway over the public road leading from Caerphilly to Quakers Yard, and terminating in the Gelligaer Common, in the parish of Gelligaer, at a point 167 yards or thereabouts, measured in a northerly direction from the north-west corner of the enclosure numbered 1707 on the 1/2500 Ordnance map of the parish of Gelligaer, and 177 yards or thereabouts, measured in a westerly direction from the north-west corner of the enclosure numbered 1718 on the said map.

2. To authorise the purchase and taking of the following pieces of land, or such part or parts thereof as may be required for the intended railway and works, which land is, or is reputed to be, common or commonable land, viz.:—

Description of Common or reputed Common and Name of Parish.	Area within Limits of Deviation about	Area estimated to be required to be taken, not exceeding
Gelligaer Common, in the parish of Gelligaer	13 acres	6 acres

3. To empower the Company to purchase and take by compulsion or agreement, and to hold lands, houses, buildings, mines and minerals, and easements therein, for the purposes of the intended railway and works in the parishes aforesaid, and also to purchase or take by compulsion or agreement, and to hold for the general purposes of the undertaking of the Company, the lands hereinafter described or referred to (that is to say) certain land in the parish of S. John the Baptist, Cardiff, in the County of Glamorgan, bounded on the south and west by land of the Rhymney Railway Company, and on the

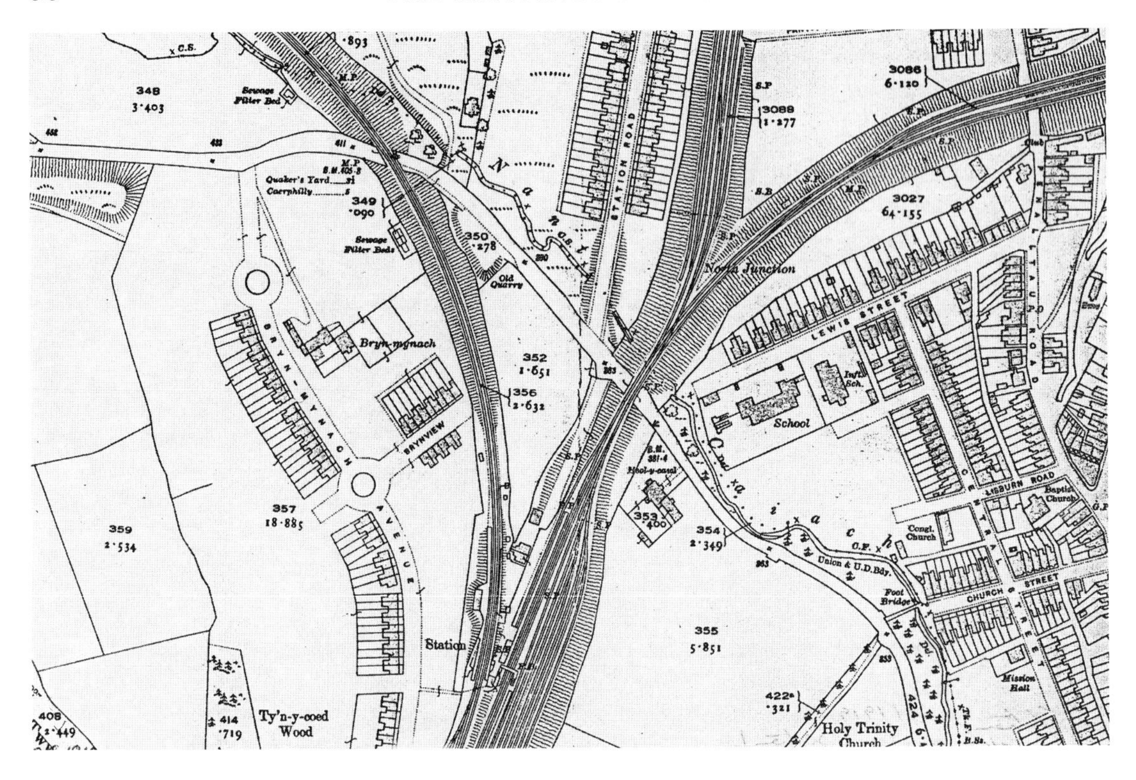

Above An Ordnance Survey map of 1919 showing Ystrad Mynach station (bottom) and the Penalltau branch spur up to the Taff Vale Extension at Penalltau Junction. North of the Caerphilly-Quakers Yard road is North Junction, the southern end of Cylla sidings and the divergence of the line up to Hengoed West Junction, with the main line going towards Hengoed (top right). *Crown copyright*

Below A 20 September 1987 photograph of North Junction, with the Cylla branch diverging left from the main line. Approaching Ystrad Mynach station is one of the then newly introduced 'Sprinters', which were gradually replacing the rather dated DMUs that had been used on these lines for more than 20 years. This example, No 150277, was placed in service in July 1987. *Author*

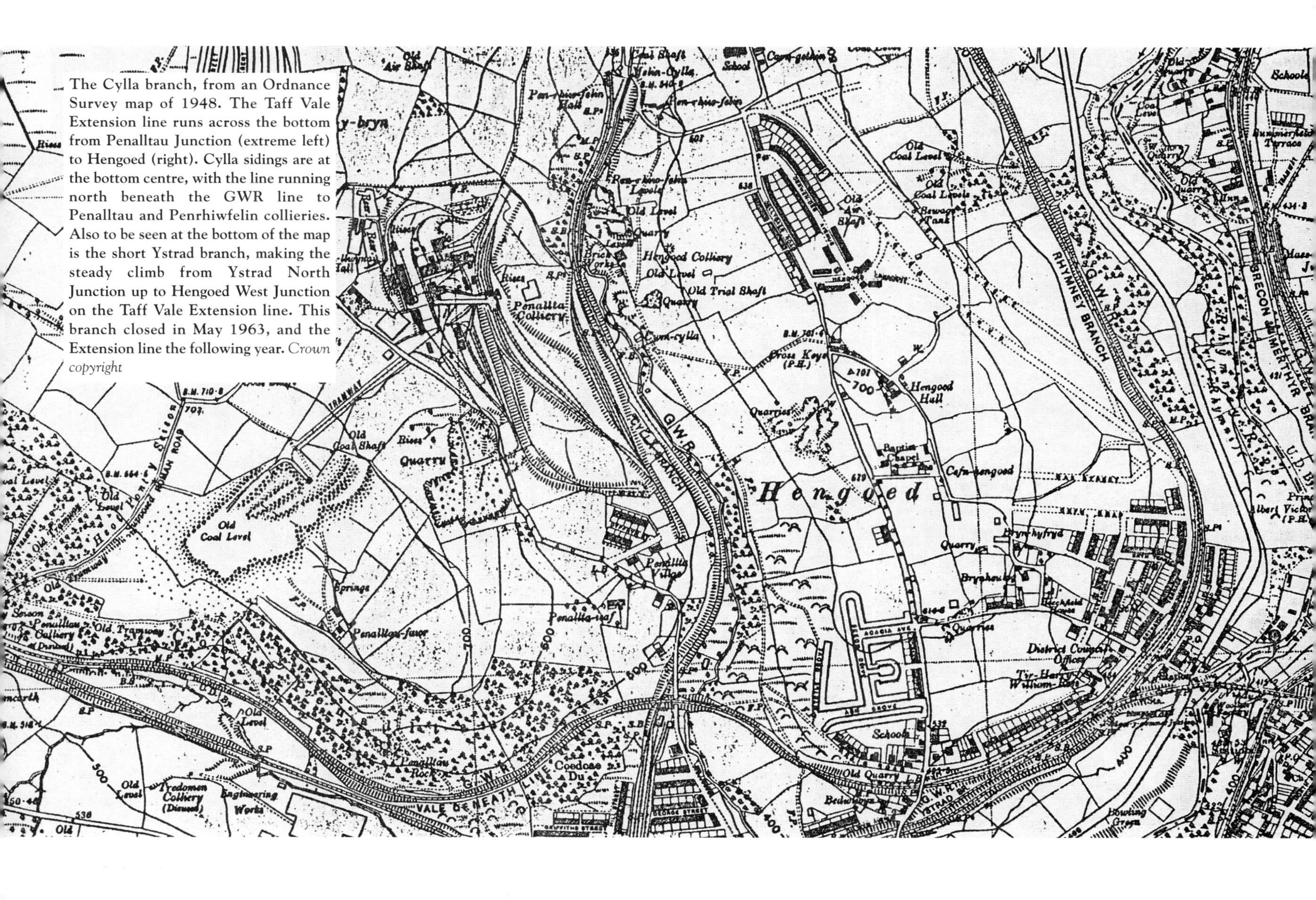

The Cylla branch, from an Ordnance Survey map of 1948. The Taff Vale Extension line runs across the bottom from Penalltau Junction (extreme left) to Hengoed (right). Cylla sidings are at the bottom centre, with the line running north beneath the GWR line to Penalltau and Penrhiwfelin collieries. Also to be seen at the bottom of the map is the short Ystrad branch, making the steady climb from Ystrad North Junction up to Hengoed West Junction on the Taff Vale Extension line. This branch closed in May 1963, and the Extension line the following year. *Crown copyright*

Above Cylla Cabin signal box at the north end of Cylla sidings, on 29 July 1960. The Taff Vale Extension line crosses in the background, and on the extreme right is the side wall of the goods shed. The signalman is keeping a careful eye on the photographer – perhaps he may be going to say something to him. *M. Hale*

Below Former Rhymney Railway 'R' Class No 42, GWR No 38, heads a down freight train towards Cylla sidings on 7 September 1957. It is about to pass beneath the Taff Vale Extension line, and the roof of Cylla Cabin can be seen just to the right of the bridge. Note the 'somersault' signal in the bottom left-hand corner. This engine was built in 1921 at the Hudswell Clarke Works as works number 1439. *B. J. Miller collection*

Above Seen from beneath the bridge on which the previous photograph was taken, former GWR 0-6-2T No 6641 is shunting near Cylla Cabin on the same day. The Rhymney Railway 'somersault' signal can be seen again. This engine was built in 1928, and withdrawn in 1962. *B. J. Miller collection*

Below Penrhiwfelin signal box was photographed on 11 July 1959, on the occasion of a Stephenson Locomotive Society visit to the branch. Seen in the background is Penalltau Colliery, as the railways knew it, although the colliery company spelled it 'Penallta'. *J. J. Davis*

Above The SLS railtour standing near Penrhiwfelin signal box on 11 July 1959. *J. J. Davis*

Left Penalltau Colliery in its last years on 20 September 1987. A former GWR pannier tank, No 7114, built in 1930 by Kerr Stuart & Co, works number 4449, was withdrawn by BR and sold to the NCB in 1959; after working at this colliery for 14 years, it was purchased for preservation and transferred from the colliery to the Severn Valley Railway on 30 March 1973. *Author*

Left This is the site of the former Penrhiwfelin Colliery Halt in 1973. Today most of the track leading to the collieries on this line has been lifted, and what remains is gradually being taken over by nature. *B. Morris*

ORDNANCE SURVEY REFERENCES

These Ordnance Survey map reference numbers are included for those readers who may wish to try and trace the locations of the bridges, halts, junctions and stations featured in these books. As mentioned elsewhere, quite a number have now disappeared under new developments, and in some cases I feel that I may have been one of the last to see the now obliterated sites.

Main line, Cardiff-Rhymney

Cardiff, Parade Station ST188767
Cardiff, Crwys Goods Station and Salisbury Road Sidings ST187769
Cardiff, Lowther Road bridge ST187773
Cardiff, Crwys Road bridge ST186778
Cardiff, Crwys Sidings ST186780 to ST185783
Cardiff, Monthermer Road bridge ST185784
Bridge plaque reads 'Eastwood Swingler and Co, London and Derby, 1909'
Cardiff, Fairoak Road bridge (*'No 18'*) ST185788
Cardiff, Cemetery Halt ST184786
Cardiff, Fairoak Siding and coal yard ST184786
Cardiff, Wedal Road railway bridge ST185782
A 48 trunk road railway bridge ST184789
The original railway bridge crossed the Taff Vale Railway at this point
Heath Junction ST182798
Heath High Level Halt ST181804
Three Arches Viaduct ST183803 to ST181816
Llanishen station ST181822
Llanishen station road bridge ST181821
Llanishen road bridge to Mill Farm ST181823
Cherry Orchard Sidings ST179834 to ST179831
Lisvane & Thornhill station (BR) ST179834
Cherry Orchard road bridge (*'No 29'*) ST179835
Cefn On Sidings ST179839 to ST179838
Cefn On Halt ST179841
Caerphilly Tunnel, south portal at Cefn On ST179843
Caerphilly Tunnel, north portal at Wernddu ST172859
Wernddu Brickworks ST168863
National Coal Board Tar Plant Siding ST169863
Caerphilly Engine and Carriage Works ST161865 to ST168865
Caerphilly station, East Junction (Brecon & Merthyr line) ST159865
Caerphilly station ST157866
Caerphilly station, West Junction (Caerphilly branch) ST153866
Aber Halt (previously Beddau Halt) ST149869
Walnut Tree Bridge Junction (at Aber Sidings) ST148873
Energlyn Colliery ST149885
Energlyn South Junction ST149878
Energlyn Mill Road bridge (*'No 39'*) ST149876
Energlyn Interchange Sidings (with Barry Railway) ST149884
Energlyn goods shed ST149878
Energlyn cattle pens ST149881
Energlyn Sidings, pedestrian underpass ST149879
Pwll-y-pant station ST149889
Llanbradach Viaduct (remains of Barry Railway viaduct over line) ST147891
Pwll-y-pant Quarry railway bridge (*'No 42'*) ST147895
Llanbradach station ST147901
Llanbradach goods shed ST148900
Llanbradach Colliery ST148908
Llanbradach Colliery Sidings ST148905 to ST149910
Ystrad Mynach Sidings ST140939 to ST142943
Ystrad Mynach South Junction (line to Penalltau Junction) ST140939
Ystrad Mynach station ST141942
Ystrad Mynach North Junction (for Cylla branch) ST143944
Hengoed Interchange Sidings (with Taff Vale Extension) ST153949
Hengoed station ST153949
Pengam Sidings ST149973 to ST151975

Pengam station ST150975
Plaque on station footbridge reads 'No 59, Finch and Co', c1900
Gilfach Fargoed Halt
(railmotor platform) ST152991
Bargoed South Junction ST152998
Bargoed station (road bridge '*No 67*') SO151000
Bargoed North Junction SO150002
Bargoed Viaduct ('*No 69*') SO150003
Cefn Brithdir Colliery Junction SO153019
Cefn Brithdir Colliery SO154016
Brithdir station SO152019
Brithdir goods shed SO152019
George Inn station SO152020
Tirphil, James Street bridge ('*No 73*') SO140032
Tirphil station SO140032
Tirphil goods shed SO139034
New Tredegar Colliery Branch
Junction SO137037
Pontlottyn station SO118061
Pontlottyn Viaduct
('*No 81*') SO116064 to SO117062
Rhymney Merthyr Colliery is now a factory, and Reed's Paper Mill covers the site
Rhymney engine shed SO111074
Rhymney station SO111074
Rhymney Diesel Sub Depot SO111074

Bute East Dock branch

This branch has been completely demolished due to the redevelopment of Cardiff's docks.
Cardiff, Crockherbtown Junction ST188767
Cardiff, Adam Street Goods Depot ST190765
Cardiff, Goal Lane Sdgs ST190765 to ST191765
Rhymney Railway
Viaduct ST193763 to ST193760
This crossed Windsor Road and Tyndall Field Sidings of the GWR, all demolished
Junction for lines to east and west
sides of Bute East Dock ST193760
Viaduct carrying Rhymney Railway
traffic to west side of
Bute East Dock ST193760 to ST194758
Sidings at north end
of East Dock ST194758 to ST194759
Bute East Dock ST193759 to ST193745

Walnut Tree branch

This was the initial main line, but when Wernddu Brickworks Siding was extended via the newly opened Caerphilly Tunnel it formed a more direct main line to Cardiff. Thereafter the Walnut Tree line, which had previously enabled Rhymney Railway traffic to reach Cardiff via the Taff Vale Railway, was reduced to branch-line status.
Walnut Tree Bridge Junction,
Taffs Well (junction '*No 12*') ST125831
Walnut Tree Bridge, Rhymney
engine shed ST125831
Railway bridge over A470 trunk road,
and site of Glamorgan Canal ST125835
Railway bridge over former
Cardiff Railway line ST125836
Rhymney Cottages railway bridge
(at Ty Rhiw) ST125837
Penrhos Junction (with Barry Railway,
opened 1926) ST138861
Penrhos Junction (with PC&N
Railway, opened 1884) ST138861
Barry Railway Viaduct, remains over
Rhymney Railway ST136860
Caerphilly Branch Junction at Penrhos
(leading to Watford Junction) ST139862
Beddau Loop Junction ST141865
Beddau Sidings ST142867 to ST144869
Caerphilly station ST148871
Site of first station, at rear of Station Inn on Nantgarw Road
Walnut Tree Bridge Junction, at
Aber Sidings ST148873

Caerphilly branch

Penrhos Junction ST138861
Beddau Loop Junction ST141865
Watford Crossing Junction ST143863
Caerphilly West Junction ST153866

Darran and Deri branch

Bargoed North Junction SO150003
Ogilvie Colliery Halt unable to trace
Groesfaen Colliery SO134007
Groesfaen Colliery Sdgs SO137004 to SO132009
Darran & Deri station SO128017
Darran & Deri goods yard and shed SO129016
Deri Junction SO126022
Darran and Deri road bridge
(Grade 3 listed) SO125025
End-on junction with Brecon & Merthyr Railway at this point

Penalltau branch

Ystrad Mynach South Junction ST140939
Ystrad Mynach station, Dowlais platform ST142942
Tredomen Junction (for Tredomen Colliery and NCB engineering works) ST139947
Penalltau Junction (with Taff Vale Extension Railway) ST128952

Rhymney Bridge branch (RR&LNWR Joint)

Butetown Road bridge SO104094
Rhymney Bridge station SO105095
Site of station now a roundabout on A465 trunk road
Nantybwch station SO131107
Station has been landscaped over, with a children's play area on the site

Taff Bargoed branch (RR&GWR Joint)

Taff Bargoed Branch Junction (at Nelson & Llancaiach) ST108965
Trelewis Platform ST105975
Taff Merthyr Colliery workers' halt ST104994
Nantwen Colliery (near Cwmfelin) SO099004
Bedlinog station SO094012
Bedlinog Colliery SO096013
Bedlinog Colliery workers' halt unable to trace
Bedlinog Colliery Sdgs S0096012 to SO096013
Cwmbargoed Pits SO093059
Rail bridge over A4060 trunk road SO069071
Zig Zag Line Junction, or Ivor Junction SO073076
Marked as 'Dowlais Junction' on Ordnance Survey maps
Dowlais Iron Works Junction SO070074
Dowlais Cae Harris station SO071079
Dowlais Cae Harris engine shed SO071079
Dowlais Cae Harris Siding (with Dowlais Iron Works) SO071078
Zig Zag Line branch junction SO069071
From this junction to Fos-y-Fran signal box, the line climbed in stages to reach a junction with the Dowlais Railway at Incline Top

Abercanaid branch (RR&GWR Joint)

Quakers Yard Viaduct (RR&GWR Joint) over River Taff ST083969
Merthyr Vale Junction ST079979 to ST078185
Embankment and viaduct over River Taff leading to Merthyr Vale Colliery and Sidings
Aberfan station ST072998
Aberfan station road bridge (*'Brymbo, 1884'*) ST072998
Aberfan station goods shed ST072997
Troedyrhiw Halt SO068018
Abercanaid station SO052039
Abercanaid station road bridge (*'Brymbo, 1884'*) SO052039
Abercanaid Siding ST052039 to SO053038
Upper Abercanaid Junction SO049043
Joint Line Junction (with Brecon & Merthyr Railway) SO050052
Merthyr High Street station SO050061
Rhymney Railway had running powers from Joint Line Junction over Brecon & Merthyr line into Merthyr High Street station

Aber branch

Aber Junction ST149875
Aber Sidings ST148877 to ST145878
Barry Railway Viaduct (over sidings) ST145878
Now part of A468 trunk road
Penyrheol Sidings ST144878 to ST142879
Penyrheol Halt ST141879
Abertridwr station and siding ST121891
Egwysilan road bridge ST119893
Windsor Colliery ST118898
Windsor Colliery South Junction, to sidings ST119894
Windsor Colliery North Junction, to sidings ST118899
Senghenydd, Station Terrace road bridge ST115907
Senghenydd Sidings ST115906 to ST113912
Senghenydd station and engine shed ST114908
A housing estate now covers former site of colliery, sidings and station

Cylla (Penrhiwfelin) branch

Ystrad Mynach North Junction ST143944
Pant-y-ceryn Street railway bridge ST143946
Taff Vale Extension Railway Viaduct (remains of) ST143949
Penalltau Colliery Sidings ST141959 to ST143954
Penrhiwfelin workmen's halt ST141961
Penrhiwfelin Colliery unable to trace

Ystrad branch

Ystrad Mynach North Junction ST143944
Hengoed West Junction ST143949

ACKNOWLEDGEMENTS

I must thank Alun Powell for finding the time to write the Foreword, and his good wife Val for being such an excellent hostess.

I would also like to thank the many people whom I have met, and express appreciation for the warm letters and treasured photographs that have been sent; I am grateful for the chance to copy and return them. Thanks also to those photographers who set out in all kinds of weather to capture a scene that nobody but a few realised would change as much as it has. I have tried to record the scene of today, and mix it with memories of the past, but without the help of others, and the guidance of our libraries and museums, the task would have been impossible.

Thanks, therefore, to the following individuals: Mr L. D. Bryant, Bridgend; Mr A. Burton (Pontypridd Public Library); Mr H. Bux (Oddfellows Club, Cardiff); Mr R. S. Carpenter, Birmingham (Lens of Sutton collection); Mr A. Carreg, Aberamen; Mr R. M. Casserley, Berkhamsted; Mr C. Chapman, Hinckley; Mr T. D. Chapman, Aberamen; Mr V. Crabb, Pontypridd; Mr J. J. Davis, Torquay; Mr M. Davies, Merthyr Tydfil; Mr J. Dore Dennis, Westra; Mr R. L. Edwards (Cardiff Public Library); Mr M. Farquhar, Portland; Mr D. A. Francis (Merthyr Tydfil Public Library); Mr M. Hale, Dudley; Mr C. W. Harris, Porth; Mrs Y. M. Harris (Caerphilly County Borough Council); Mrs E. Hart (Illustrated London News Library, London); Mr J. C. Haydon, Reading; Mr B. Hoper, Insch (The Transport Secretary); Mr F. T. Hornby, North Cheam; Mr C. Hughes, Abercynon; Mr G. James (Merthyr Tydfil Public Library); Mr D. K. Jones, Mountain Ash; Mr H. F. Jones, Pontlottyn; Mr P. Korrison, St Albans; Mr H. Leadbetter, Upton Wirral; Mr M. E. Ling (Cardiff Public Library); Mrs H. Lloyd Fernandez (ABP, Cardiff); Mr M. Lloyd, Hereford; Mr B. J. Miller, Barry; Mr J. Morgan, Cardiff; Mr B. Morris, Merthyr Tydfil; Mrs J. E. Overall, Caterham; Mr M. O'Connel, GWR Staff Assoc Club, Cardiff; Mr G. Pearce, Cardiff; Mr S. C. L. Phillips, c/o Mr D. K. Jones, Mountain Ash; Mr A. Powell, Rhydyfelin; Mr K. Ryan, Pontypridd; Mrs S. Scott (Rhondda Borough Libraries); Mr G. W. Sharpe, Barnsley; Mrs J. Smith, (Associated British Ports, Cardiff); Mr G. Stacey, Egham (RAS Marketing, LCGB Collection); Mr E. J. Starr, Caerphilly; Mr C. Thomas (Deputy Port Manager, ABP, Cardiff); Mr D. G. Thomas, London; Mr T. Underwood (Oddfellows Club, Cardiff); Mr D. Watkins, Merthyr Tydfil; and Mrs E. Williams, Caerphilly.

Thanks also to: Caerphilly Public Library; Cardiff Public Library; Cynon Valley Libraries; Great Western Railway Staff Association Club, Cardiff; Great Western Railway Staff Association Club, Merthyr Tydfil; Merthyr Tydfil Public Libraries; Mid Glamorgan Libraries; Locomotive Club of Great Britain; Locomotive and General Railway Photographs Company; Oddfellows Club, Cardiff; Ordnance Survey Department, Southampton; Real Photographs Company, Weybridge; Rhondda Borough Libraries; South Glamorgan Libraries, for permission to use extracts from the *Cardiff & Merthyr Guardian*.

Thanks to Mr G. Body of Avon Anglia Publications, for permission to use the late C. R. Clinker's register of closed stations and halts, also with the permission of the widow of the late C. R. Clinker.

To Mr G. G. Jones, for his permission to use extracts from his thesis on the history of Caerphilly, with reference to the collieries in the Rhymney Valley, extracts from the Journal of the Caerphilly Local History Society, and extracts he kindly sent me from his *Cronicl Caerffili* Nos 5 and 6, and from the *Cardiff Times*.

To Mr Kichenside, editor, David & Charles publishers, for permission to use opening and closing dates of stations.

To the editor of the Illustrated London News Library, London, for permission to use the sketch of the Bute East Dock Extension.

To the editor of the Oakwood Press, for permission to use opening dates of stations, halts and junctions from the excellent work by Mr D. S. M. Barrie.

To Mr J. Slater, of *The Railway Magazine*, for his permission to use extracts and captions from the 1910, 1912, 1923 and 1924 editions of the magazine.

To Mr R. A. Storey and M. A. G. Tough, of the University of Warwick Library and Modern Records Centre, and to the Secretary of the National Union of Railwaymen, London, for their permission to use the TVR strike telegram of 1900.

To Joyce, widow of the late Norman Browne, of Surrey, a gentleman and a good railway photographer.

To the memory of Mr Glyn Davies of Aberdare, a good local, historical and industrial photographer.

To the widow of the late John A. Owen, for the use of his photographic collection on Dowlais Works.

To the widow of the late Norman Parry, a member of the GWR Staff Association Club, Merthyr Tydfil.

To the memory of Mr John Phelps, former employee of ABP, Cardiff, a good man and friend to all.

To the widow of the late Sid Rickard, another gentleman, whose passing marks the end of an era.

To the memory of Mr John Smith, of Lens of Sutton, another sad loss, but whose collection lives on.

INDEX